CHATTERBOXES

'In 1949 in a desperately close Boat Race John Snagge made his best-known "gaffe": ". . . it's a very close race – I can't see who is in the lead – it's either Oxford or Cambridge!"'

'Wynford Vaughan-Thomas was once the commentator at a television outside broadcast from a steel works. As a white-hot rod of steel passed him along a conveyor belt he shouted above the din of the works, "Here comes thirty foot of white-hot steel, untouched by human hand!"'

'When commentating for radio outside St Paul's Cathedral for the wedding of Prince Charles and Lady Diana I found myself saying: "I can see the bride's procession coming up Ludgate Hill. When she arrives below me here at St Paul's she will walk with her father up the steps into the pavilion – er – I mean Cathedral."'

Brian Johnston joined the BBC's Outside Broadcasts Department immediately after the war, and his affectionate and humorous account of the commentators and their art is permeated with his own deep knowledge, wide experience and love of broadcasting.

Also available in Star

IT'S A FUNNY GAME
IT'S BEEN A LOT OF FUN

CHATTERBOXES

My Friends the Commentators

Brian Johnston

A STAR BOOK

published by
the Paperback Division of
W. H. ALLEN & Co. PLC

A Star Book
Published in 1984
by the Paperback Division of
W. H. Allen & Co. PLC
44 Hill Street, London W1X 8LB

First published in Great Britain by Methuen London Ltd, 1983

Reprinted 1987, 1988.

Copyright © Brian Johnston, 1983

Printed and bound in Great Britain by
Cox & Wyman Ltd, Reading

ISBN 0 352 31493 1

Acknowledgements

I should like to acknowledge with gratitude the help given to me by 'Lobby' de Lotbinière, Charles Max-Muller, John Snagge, Don Mosey, the BBC Reference Library, the BBC News Information Service and the BBC Written Archives Centre (Caversham). My thanks also to Diana Fisher, who gave me the idea of the title as we sunbathed on a beach at Sydney Harbour.

Contents

Introduction

On Saturday 27 December 1980 I was invited to be the studio guest in BBC Radio 2's *Sport on 2* programme. During the afternoon the presenter, Mike Ingham, suggested that I might like to try out his job, and cue over to the commentator at the various sporting events around the country. I did not do it very well, but I thoroughly enjoyed myself because I found that I knew them all personally. After the programme it dawned on me that I not only just knew, but had probably worked with, all the television and radio commentators who had broadcast from the time when I joined the BBC in 1946.

So I thought it would be fun – at least for me – to look back on my thirty-seven years of broadcasting and recall the characters and techniques of some of my colleagues, not forgetting the slight mishaps or gaffes which have occurred. But there will be no sensational revelations. This book will be just an appreciation – in both senses of the word – of 'my friends the commentators'.

Awards

Best Broadcaster	Richard Dimbleby
Best All-rounder	John Snagge
Best Television Sports Commentator	Henry Longhurst
Best Radio Sports Commentator	John Arlott
Most Adjectival	Peter Jones
Most Beguiling	Gerald Williams
Most Confident	David Coleman
Most Dependable	Peter West
Most Effervescent	Wynford Vaughan-Thomas
Fastest Talkers	Max Robertson ⎫ Peter Bromley ⎬
The Least-Known Face Among the Top Television Commentators	Bill McLaren
Most Loquacious	Henry Blofeld
Most Lucid	Raymond Baxter
Most Modest	Brian Moore
Most Painstaking in Research and Preparation	Robert Hudson
Most Royal	Tom Fleming
Most Versatile Sports Commentator	Raymond Glendenning

Part One Early Days

CHAPTER 1

Lobby

I joined the BBC only in January 1946, but there had of course been broadcasting for a quarter of a century before that. This was during my school and university days and, although not a regular listener, I did tune in to the wireless for sport and entertainment. I enjoyed comedians like Tommy Handley, Clapham and Dwyer, and Gillie Potter, and at night listened to the dance bands in their weekly spots from the great London hotels – names like Ambrose, Harry Roy, Caroll Gibbons, Roy Fox, Sidney Lipton and Lew Stone.

So far as sport was concerned I was always fascinated by the 'live' broadcasts of something which was actually happening at the time. The men who described the sports became my unseen heroes. They were the pioneers of commentary and each in his own style left a deep impression on me: R. C. Lyle on racing, Captain H. B. T. Wakelam on rugby and lawn tennis, George Allison on football and Howard Marshall on cricket. Except for the latter I never met any of them, so I thought that it would be a good way to start by finding out more about them as people and broadcasters, and also about the great difficulties which they had to overcome in the early days of Outside Broadcasts: I am indebted to three people especially for 'filling me in' about this pre-war period in radio and television commentary. First, my original boss S. J. de Lotbinière, known to everybody as 'Lobby' and who bears a heavy responsibility for taking me on at the BBC. My second boss was Charles Max-Muller who had been General Manager of Outside Broadcasts ('O.B.s', as they are called) in the thirties, and I am most grateful too to him and to John Snagge for their picture of what broadcasting was like before the war.

Lobby became Head of O.B.s in 1935, taking over from Gerald Cock who had formed the O.B. Department in 1925. In 1952 he went over to do the same thing on television. Lobby had taken a degree in Law at Cambridge and came into the BBC with no technical or sporting qualifications. He started in 'Talks', and because no one else wanted it, was given a Saturday-afternoon sports programme to produce. It was in no way like the slick *Sport on 2* which we now enjoy every Saturday, when we are whisked from commentary point to commentary point all over Great Britain, and even all over the world.

Lobby's programme was largely in the studio with interviews and discussion, with just the occasional O.B. thrown in as an extra bonus. But the programme did introduce Lobby to many of the prominent sportsmen and administrators of the day. These gave him the vital contacts which were of such value to him in later years, when he had to negotiate broadcasts for sporting events.

There was then virtually no commentary as we know it today. There had been sporting broadcasts since January 1927, but they were more often than not just eye-witness accounts, reports or summaries at an interval, half-time or close of play. There were exceptions such as the occasional horse race, the Boat Race and snatches of rugby, tennis, soccer and cricket. What commentary there was, was done by experts in the particular sport, without any training as broadcasters. For instance, R. C. Lyle was *The Times'* racing correspondent and, although he was a great race-reader and judge of a race, he gave none of the colourful description which we get today, nor did he name all the horses in the race. That is what the listener wants to know – how *his* horse is doing, however badly.

One of the troubles was that there were so few races broadcast – just the big ones – that people like R. C. Lyle had no practice in the art of commentary. Nor had they time to learn from the BBC what that art was. It was the same with George Allison. He was a great authority on soccer, but with no training found it difficult to give a clear picture of the run of play or where the ball was.

A different type of broadcaster was Captain H. B. T.

(Teddy) Wakelam who had played rugby for the Harlequins. He in fact gave the very first live sporting commentary in this country. It came from Twickenham during the England *v* Wales match on 15 January 1927. From this he spread his wings to soccer, tennis and even cricket. He was a good talker and always ready to learn. I say, 'even cricket', because he was not the first to broadcast on that game. That honour fell to P. F. Warner – 'Plum' – later Sir Pelham. On 14 May 1927 he was at Leyton to 'describe' Essex *v* New Zealand. He had a very quiet and rather ineffectual, apologetic-sounding voice and was not a great success.

He was followed later in the same year by the Essex player Canon F. H. Gillingham (Gilly). Gilly was a fine preacher with a strong authoritative voice. But, alas, he did not do too well either. He was also at Leyton but unfortunately his first broadcast coincided with a twenty-minute interval. After he had given a ten-minute description of the play so far, he became desperate for something to say. There was no Bill Frindall to talk to about records in those days. So the poor Canon read out the advertisements round the ground. You can imagine the reaction of the BBC in those days. Advertising in any form was strictly forbidden. Even in the 1950s I remember we were doing a broadcast about the motor industry, and we had to say that we were speaking from a well-known car factory at Dagenham. Thank goodness things are far more relaxed today.

So Lobby realized that he had to train people to be broadcasters first and foremost. It was no good having an expert who could not communicate with the listener, nor describe what was happening on the field. Of course the mix had to be right. The broadcaster must have knowledge of the sport which he was describing, and should certainly have played it or participated in it. He could then have an international sportsman alongside him as a summarizer who would give expert comment as opposed to commentary. Early examples of these were Arthur Gilligan at cricket, Harold Abrahams at athletics and Bernard Darwin at golf.

The first thing Lobby decided to do was to abandon the 'square one' technique which was in existence when he took over. This enabled the listener to follow a game of rugby or soccer by looking at a plan in the *Radio Times* in which the playing area was divided up into numbered squares. The commentator would have a second person in the box with him whose job was to follow the ball and call out the numbered square in which it was. John Snagge was often called on to do this, and as you can imagine his interruptions frequently interfered with the commentary, as there were two voices speaking at once.

Lobby decided that a good commentator must be able to place the ball by his description – 'the ball is on the England 25 line on the far side of the field', or 'the ball has gone out five yards short of Arsenal's right-corner flag'. For a commentator to be able to do this there had to be a definite commentary technique laid down, and so Lobby evolved his now universally accepted Pyramid Method. In this the commentator starts his broadcast at the narrow top of the pyramid by giving straight away the main essentials. Then gradually as the broadcast continues, the commentator broadens outwards by giving less important but still necessary information.

At any game, for instance, a commentator must immediately give the score and say how much time is left or, in the case of limited-over cricket, how many overs are left. At this stage too he should name the goal scorers, or which batsmen are out and how many runs they have each made.

Once this has been done he should set the scene – the weather, the crowd, the condition of the ground or pitch, and where he is sitting in relation to the play. He will then find time to say who won the toss, give the teams and describe briefly any outstanding play by any particular player.

Then can come what is called the 'associative material' – the position of the two sides in the League or Championship Tables, how important this match is for them, likely landmarks for any player, for example his thousand runs for the season or a significant number of goals. When time allows the commentator should always try to weave in a description of the ground, and once again place the position of his commentary box. He is after all the eyes of the listener, who can then imagine that the armchair in which he is sitting is on the balcony of the Lord's pavilion or in some gallery high up in St Paul's Cathedral.

One other important thing to remember is to repeat essential information from time to time, such as a cricket score-card or who has scored the goals. New listeners or viewers are continually switching on, and not only do they expect to hear the current score almost immediately but also details of what has happened. To the commentator it often sounds repetitive, but to the newcomer it is just what is wanted. In limited-over cricket too the commentator should turn himself into a human calculator, and regularly inform listeners how many runs are still needed for victory and how many overs are left.

Lobby also added some 'Do's' and 'Don'ts' for commentators:

Do's

1 Always try to build up 'suspense interest', anticipating possible interesting or exciting happenings to come. Enthusiasm for his subject is vital for a commentator but he should never *over* build up a match or event. He soon loses his credibility if he does, especially in radio, since the listener can now often check up on the television.

2 There is also a place for a certain amount of subtle instruction in sport, especially on television. But it must be done casually and not in too schoolmasterly a manner. There is so much that can be explained to the inexpert viewer or listener – the no-ball law, the intricacies of a tie-break at lawn tennis or the reasons for a foul at football.

Don'ts

1 However badly unsighted, try never to say, 'I can't see.' It is natural to think of an excuse if someone gets in your line of vision, or a player runs into a corner of the ground which you cannot see from the commentary box. But it becomes boring for the listener who rightly believes that for his licence fee the BBC should site the box properly, though this is not always possible due to structural difficulties. Similarly some boxes are often cramped, too hot or too cold, and desperately uncomfortable. However, that is not the listeners' fault and they soon become tired of constant moaning.

2 Never take sides. Be completely impartial – something far more easily said than done. The temptation to say 'we' is very strong but inexcusable, even when broadcasting from an overseas tour, when you get the feeling of representing your country. It's so easy to say, 'You'll be glad to hear that Brearley has won the toss,' when of course some listeners will *not* be glad. I know I must have been guilty many times of putting too much obvious delight into my shout of 'He's out!' when 'he' happens to be Australia's best batsman.

There was one bit of advice which Lobby gave his commentators which has on occasions been slightly misinterpreted. In an unguarded moment he once said that every commentator should soak himself in his subject. Some of them did – and do!

By following the Pyramid Method a commentator will acquire a certain rhythm: essential information – associative material – build-up of suspense – repetition for new listeners – a bit of instruction – and a final neat summary of what has happened to bring the commentary to an end. I can perhaps best explain this sense of rhythm from my experience as a cricket commentator.

The one cardinal sin is to miss a ball. So funny stories, explanation of laws, quiz questions, assessment of the game's position must all be kept for those many pauses which occur during a game of cricket – the time between overs, the fast bowler's long walk back to his mark, injuries, drinks, changing of the ball and crowd interruptions. But once the bowler gets back to his mark all this *must* stop.

The commentator should then describe: the bowler running up, his approach to the umpire, his delivery, the type of ball, its length and where it pitched.

Then (if he hits the ball) should come the batsman's stroke, where the ball has gone, who is fielding or chasing it, and how many runs the batsmen are running.

Finally when the ball has been returned to the wicket-keeper or bowler and thus become 'dead', the commentator must say how many runs have been added and give the new totals both for the team and the batsman.

Then and only then should the commentator talk about

anything else until the bowler reaches his mark. Then back into the rhythm again.

After reading all this I hope that the young would-be commentator is not too disheartened. It appears to make the job of commentary more difficult than it really is, and to make out commentators to be a superbreed of men. Of course they aren't. But they are at least an *unusual* breed.

The early commentators were having to learn as they went along, with only Lobby to lean on for advice. They could not, as we could, get help from an older commentator – there just weren't any. The conditions under which they worked were appalling by modern standards. They were crammed into a small wooden box either at the back of a grandstand or on top of a van. Sometimes at the Derby they had to broadcast sitting or standing among the crowds on a stand. There is even a photograph of some unfortunate commentator at an outside broadcast at Cambridge perched microphone in hand, up a tree. Mind you, some of our positions are fairly primitive today, but luxurious compared to forty years ago. Their style of dress cannot have helped much either, and in almost every photograph commentators are wearing 'Anthony Eden' Homburg hats – what they did with the headphones goodness only knows.

Then of course they did not have the motorways and Inter-City expresses. A journey which today takes us only three hours could have taken double or even more before the war. And if things went wrong – especially on overseas broadcasts – communications were no way near as good as they are today. Lobby himself found this out when over in Holland for the wedding of Princess Juliana in the late thirties. The timings for the procession and the service went hopelessly wrong and it became obvious that everything was running at least half an hour late. Today a commentator could dial the number of Broadcasting House in London, and ask them to delay the broadcast. But Lobby could not get through to warn them, so when they came over as advertised he had to waffle for at least half an hour before anything happened. Luckily he had practised what he preached and had plenty of associative material about Holland, their Royal Family and so on. But he admits that in the end he got so desperate that he had to resort to reading out the bulb catalogues! This became a slightly longer broadcast than the one he did from an aeroplane on the Boat Race. The plane had to cross and recross the winding River Thames and Lobby soon became violently air-sick. When John Snagge cued over to him, he just managed to splutter out, 'Cambridge in the lead by three lengths – back to the launch.' A somewhat expensive eleven words.

One other important improvement today is the equipment, which today is smaller, lighter and of far higher quality. But the thirties did see a minor revolution – the lip microphone. This was the invention of a Dr Alexander of the BBC, and meant that the commentator had to hold the microphone right up to his mouth. This enabled him to broadcast from the middle of a noisy crowd, with only his voice being heard, and no other crowd effects. It was a very important advance in the technique of commentating.

Commentary is a comparatively new art form, there having been no such thing (as we know it today) until the late 1920s, and it undoubtedly calls for a number of characteristics in anyone hoping to be a commentator. We are all, I fear, extroverts – we have to be. We *must* enjoy performing before millions of viewers or listeners, and should have a good vocabulary, powers of description and the ability to keep talking regardless of panics or mishaps – and there are plenty of those. But the most important asset of all is a distinctive and easily recognizable voice. It helps of course if it is also pleasant and friendly, and sounds confident and knowledgeable.

It does not matter whether it has either a regional accent or is a more traditional 'BBC' voice. In fact the former can be a definite advantage with some sports or occasions. But I think that it is vital in order to become a top commentator for the voice to be immediately recognizable. There are, and have been, some very efficient commentators who have no personality in their voice. Nowadays, for instance, it can be quite difficult to distinguish between the various 'mid-Atlantic' accents which are heard. I always feel that it is better for someone to say: 'Oh, there's that awful chap Brian Johnston waffling away again,' than, 'Who's that commentating? He's good. I've heard him before but can never put a name to the voice.'

I suppose the best known voices over the post-war years have been those of John Arlott with his gruff Hampshire accent, John Snagge with his deep, more orthodox 'Oxford' voice, and Terry Wogan with his Irish intonation. They have all done more radio than television, and it is obviously more difficult for an out-of-vision television commentator to put himself across.

Besides the voice, a good vocabulary, and the ability to describe what you see, a commentator must have a retentive memory, be quick-witted and have the common touch without any suspicion of pomposity. In other words he must be humble and not too 'know-all', and use, where possible, conversational, colloquial English.

Good health and a strong constitution are essential. A businessman or someone working in a factory can say, 'I'm not feeling too good. I won't go in today.' But the commentator has to be at the Test Match, horse race or cere-monial occasion. He cannot catch up on his work the next day. It has already happened. And finally a happy marriage *does* help! What better than at the end of a long exhausting day to come home to a loving wife and collapse in an arm-chair with a nice meal on a tray. Not very romantic, maybe, but a wonderful way of winding down after a day at the microphone.

CHAPTER 2

The Pre-War Pioneers

R. C. Lyle

R. C. Lyle, the racing correspondent of *The Times*, was the BBC's choice as their first racing commentator. Believe it or not he was said to be colour-blind, so how he picked out the horses I just don't know. Maybe he was so involved in racing and going to every meeting that he knew all the horses – in addition of course to the jockeys – by sight. But anyhow he was a brilliant race-reader and a superb judge of a race. As a result he often decided fairly far out from the winning post which horse was going to win, and used to call it home, hardly mentioning the other horses who were struggling for a place.

He was naturally somewhat nervous before his first big broadcast, which was when Felstead, ridden by Harry Wragg, won the Derby in 1928. On his way to the commentary position he happened to run into Edgar Wallace who, besides being a prolific writer of novels and plays, was a keen racehorse owner. He noticed that R. C. Lyle was looking a bit pale around the gills. So not very helpfully he suggested to Lyle that there was only one thing worse than having to give a commentary on such a difficult race as the Derby – and that was to be hung. However, he made amends by insisting that Lyle drank a bottle of champagne. As a result his broadcast was a great success, though I do not think that such 'medicine' would be included in Lobby's list of what a commentator needs. But from personal experience I can confirm that at least it does not do any harm!

R. C. Lyle (note that some commentators, like E. W. [Jim] Swanton in later years, preferred their initials to be used rather than their Christian names) once shocked many listeners and horrified the Director-General, Sir John Reith. In the Derby when Cameronian beat Orpen he got so excited at the distance (240 yards from the winning post) that he shouted, 'It's the *hell* of a race!' Broadcasting House was inundated with telephone calls of protest. If any of those people who rang up then were alive today, I reckon they would have a pretty hefty phone bill!

In 1938, towards the end of the Northumberland Plate, Lyle suffered a commentator's nightmare. His voice completely dried up and he was unable to broadcast the finish of the race. He was undoubtedly a great expert on racing and knew every horse, trainer, owner and jockey. But were you able to hear him today you would notice the absence of pre-race description, information about the horses, and the subtle build-up of suspense and excitement which someone like Peter Bromley gives you now. In fact Lyle really only took over the microphone when the horses were at the start, and another broadcaster – sometimes George Allison – would handle all the preliminaries.

There was one other occasion when Lyle fell foul of Sir John Reith, who was a teetotaller. During the early stages of the Derby Lyle said, 'The horses are now passing the advertisement hoarding for Booth's Dry Gin,' – this being a conspicuous landmark just after the start. Not only had he broken the BBC rules by advertising, but it was also for drink. Sir John was also not too pleased when a representative of Gordon's Gin rang up not only to protest but also to ask how they too could get in to the act!

George Allison

George Allison was a rotund, cheerful figure. He was too busy with his job as manager of Arsenal F.C. to give sufficient time to the technique of commentary. But he knew his football and all the players, and in the thirties he was the voice of soccer. He certainly had the gift of the gab. On one occasion at Loch Lomond when describing an attempt on the speedboat record, he kept going for forty minutes while he waited for Kaye Don to appear in *Miss England III*. In 1936, when Arsenal were in the Cup Final against Sheffield

United and he thought it his duty to be with them, he withdrew from the commentary. For the first time *two* commentators – Ivan Sharpe and F. N. S. Creek – did the job which George had previously done on his own.

It is interesting to note that he got little support from his fellow football administrators, who regarded the broadcasting of matches with suspicion and, often, hostility, fearing the effect it would have on their gates. The matches on which George Allison commentated were all connected with the Football Association. The Football League steadfastly refused the BBC permission to broadcast any League matches before the war. At one time the clubs voted not only to bar commentary of the F.A. Cup Final but also against the players being numbered. What a nightmare that would be for a football commentator! It only emphasizes the difficulties of doing commentary in those days. So George Allison was restricted to Cup Ties and international matches and was never a regular commentator every Saturday.

During the war Alan Hardacre, the League Secretary, relented and League matches were broadcast for the Forces. After the war Lobby managed with difficulty to obtain permission to broadcast League matches on a regular basis every Saturday. But there was one stipulation. Until they cued over to the commentator on the ground, the BBC was not allowed to announce where the match was being held. In fact to start with it was made a complete mystery and the studio would cue over to Raymond Glendenning with something along the lines of, 'And now it's time for our soccer commentary on one of today's League matches. Our commentator is Raymond Glendenning so over to him now to find out where he is.' It was not until some years later that the studio was allowed to say which match it was in their cue over to Raymond. There is still a restriction today. *Sport on 2* is not allowed to say which match is being broadcast until 3 p.m.

George came from Stockton-on-Tees and was a friendly, jolly and popular man. He was a very hard worker and although he could be tough, he always *cared* for his players at Arsenal. It is probably not generally known that he once scooped an interview with Lord Kitchener for the American newspaper magnate Randolph Hearst, and as a result became his press representative in the United Kingdom.

Even in those days before television his voice and face were easily recognized. Once at a railway station a porter approached him and said, 'Excuse me asking you sir, but are you the gentleman what radiates?'

Once when he had remarked that he found it difficult to see over the heads of the crowd, a listener wrote to him suggesting that he gave his commentary from a balloon! There was also the lady who kept a parrot which was normally a very quiet and well behaved bird. But there was something about George's voice which stirred it to strong language. Whenever George shouted, 'It's a goal, it's a goal,' the parrot would pipe up, 'Damn you – shut up, you old bugger!'

Tommy Woodroffe

Commander Tommy Woodroffe was the only commentator ever to have a West End show named after him – George Black's *The Fleet's Lit Up* at the Hippodrome (later The Talk of the Town). In fact, in spite of the many good things he did, his name will always be connected with that famous broadcast from the Royal Naval Review at Spithead in 1935. It was very bad luck on him because he had to spend all day of the broadcast aboard his old ship, H.M.S. *Nelson*, and among his old shipmates. They were over-hospitable to their old friend, and to make matters worse, they treated the BBC official who was there to look after the Commander in the same way. The result was that by the time dusk fell and it was time for the Fleet to switch on their lights, neither were in a fit state for the broadcast.

I suppose that many people today have never either heard the broadcast, nor the recording. It is certainly one of the classics of broadcasting. Here is an extract from it, and it was delivered, as you can imagine, in a slurred voice, slowly and deliberately.

> . . . The Fleet's lit up. When I say 'lit up' I mean lit up by fairy lights. It's lit up by fairy lights . . . it isn't a

Fleet at all . . . the whole Fleet is a Fairyland. If you follow me through . . . if you don't mind . . . when I say 'the Fleet's lit up' I mean the whole ships . . . (extra long pause) . . . I was telling someone to shut up. The whole Fleet's lit up . . . the ships are lit up . . . even the destroyers are lit up. We are going to fire a rocket . . . we are going to fire all sorts of things . . . you may hear my reaction when I see them . . . A huge Fleet here . . . a colossal Fleet all lit up with fairy lights . . . The whole thing is Fairyland . . . it isn't true . . . It's gone, it's gone . . . it's disappeared . . . No magician ever waved his wand with more acumen.

The Fleet's gone . . . it's disappeared . . . I'm trying to give you Ladies and Gentlemen a description . . . the Fleet's gone . . . it's disappeared . . . the whole thing's gone . . . They've disappeared . . . We had two hundred warships all round us . . . Now they've all gone . . . There's nothing between us and heaven . . . there's nothing at all . . .

The broadcast was then faded out with the announcer saying: 'And that is the end of our relay from Spithead, so now over to the Carlton Hotel for dance music.'

The next morning a tired and rather worse-for-wear Woodroffe reported to Lobby, who had not, unusually for him, heard the broadcast. But Broadcasting House was humming with excitement, and Lobby wisely told Woodroffe to go home and have a good sleep.

Meanwhile Sir John Reith arrived, with his beetling, black eyebrows boding no good for Woodroffe. It was bad luck for the Commander that not only was Sir John strongly against drink on any occasion, let alone at a broadcast, but also that his number two was Admiral Carpendale, a strict disciplinarian in the true naval tradition. So the anti-drink/Royal Navy combination was a formidable force. Sir John's first words to his personal assistant were, 'Has de Lotbinière suspended Woodroffe yet?' Lobby rightly had not done so, since he himself had no first-hand knowledge of what had happened, and refused to take any action until he had investigated.

However, matters were taken out of his hands, and a tribunal was set up to 'try' Woodroffe. Sir John evidently thought that the BBC owed it to the listeners to take strong action. Thanks, largely, I feel sure, to the intervention of Lobby, Woodroffe was only suspended from duty for six months. And so he retired temporarily from the microphone – the best-known broadcaster of all time.

He was in fact extremely versatile and when he returned took part in a variety of O.B.s, including ceremonials, the 1936 Olympic Games, the 1939 Derby and the 1939 F.A. Cup Final. He was once hauled over the coals for submitting a large expense sheet for hospitality without naming the lucky recipients. So after the Derby he put in his expenses once again showing a large sum for entertaining. But this time he put: '– to the Clerk of the Course, the Judge, the starter and a gentleman with glasses wearing a pin-stripe suit whose name I didn't quite catch.' And the BBC were happy!

H. B. T. Wakelam and others

There were a number of characters among the pre-war commentators. In lawn tennis there was Colonel Brand, a well-known Wimbledon linesman, who for some reason wore his Homburg hat sideways. After one of his broadcasts in 1929 the *Yorkshire Observer* wrote: 'Tennis-ear-ache! What interest does tennis hold for us? I suppose shortly we shall hear a running commentary on a ping-pong match.' Things have certainly changed fifty years later.

Like R. C. Lyle, Colonel Brand once lost his voice in the middle of a commentary. Nothing came, and he had to be faded out, as he couldn't even manage to say, 'back to the studio.' He once got very excited during a long rally: 'Smash, recovery, smash, recovery, smash, recovery, gosh – it's gone hurtling into the Royal Box at Toque height.' Whether Queen Mary had time to duck is not related.

A Canadian, Bob Bowman, used to do the ice hockey commentaries before Stewart Macpherson. During one particularly vicious and dirty game in Prague, he changed to a boxing commentary in an attempt to describe the fisticuffs out on the rink.

Michael Standing was a member of BBC staff and before the war did cricket commentary, often in partnership with Howard Marshall. He had a rather slow languid drawl, well suited to the quieter periods of cricket. He was very tall and a useful fast medium bowler, and knew his cricket.

Because of his name, John Watt, the then Head of Variety, devised a street-interview spot for him which he called 'Standing on the Corner'. Michael did commentary other than cricket, including once the Ceremony of the Keys at the Tower of London. He had just said, 'And now silence descends on Tower Hill,' when a roar of half a dozen motor-bikes rent the night air. During the war he took over the O.B. Department from Lobby and afterwards became Head of Light Entertainment. It was in this capacity that he once had to give me a rocket for allowing a rude joke to be told on the air. You can hardly believe it today, but the joke was: *Boy at school*: 'Have you seen Miss Brown, the P.T. instructress?' *Second boy*: 'Yes, she's in the gymnasium, stripped for gym.' *First boy*: 'Lucky J(g)ym!'

A highly efficient Jack-of-all-trades was Captain H. B. T. Wakelam, who soon abandoned his initials and was known as 'Teddy'. In giving the first-ever live running commentary, at Twickenham on 15 January 1927, he gained an important place in broadcasting history. At half-time he was heard to say on the air: 'What about a beer?' He deserved it!

After the match the *Spectator* reported: 'That type of broadcasting has come to stay.' How right they were. To prove his versatility Wakelam achieved another 'first' the following Saturday – the first *soccer* commentary on Arsenal *v* Sheffield United at Highbury. In 1935 he also gave ten-minute comments on the Tests against South Africa during the intervals and close of play. In 1938 he achieved yet another first – in the televising of the Lord's Test between England and Australia, his was the first-ever television commentary on cricket ever given anywhere in the world. He also commentated for television later that year at the Oval and again in 1939 for the West Indies Tests at Lord's and the Oval, assisted by Aidan Crawley and Tommy Wood-roffe.

For some reason, however, Wakelam was never enthusiastic about cricket, and thought the game quite unsuitable for lengthy descriptions of play over the air. 'It was too dull,' he said. What sacrilege! But he was not the only one to hold that opinion. After the initial experiments in 1927 of *reporting* from cricket matches the *Daily Telegraph* wrote: 'It is obviously impossible to broadcast anything but short periods of description of a three-day cricket match.' I wonder what the writer would have thought today about our five-day ball-by-ball commentaries on *Test Match Special*.

Wakelam also covered lawn tennis with Colonel Brand and there were complaints that with the Colonel, the Captain and the Commander (Woodroffe) the BBC was turning itself into a sort of Cheltenham military establishment. Once on a very hot day at Wimbledon Wakelam caused quite a sensation during his commentary on the Men's Doubles. The commentary box was full of old papers, and while lighting a cigarette he accidentally dropped the match among them. They caught fire and burnt his trousers, but he managed to stamp out the blaze without interrupting his commentary. He was one of the main pioneers of commentary and showed remarkable knowledge of all the sports which he covered. He was definitely in the top league of commentators during the last fifty years.

Howard Marshall

The pre-war commentator who made the deepest impression on me was Howard Marshall. I still remember with nostalgia hearing him describe the closing stages of Len Hutton's innings of 364 at the Oval in 1938. I was having a picnic by a river in Yorkshire with some friends, and his slow, deep, burbling voice came through loud and clear. '... Bradman with his arms akimbo, the bees are buzzing, and the Oval sparrows by the Pavilion Gate ...' It was evocative stuff and paced exactly right for cricket. I think it's fair to say that of all the pre-war commentators he would be the only one totally acceptable today, so good was his technique and his knowledge of cricket. He was a rugby blue at Oxford, but only a good class club cricketer. Unlike most of the others he was a member of the BBC staff, and so had the advantage of accumulating experience as a broadcaster. Besides cricket and rugby he did boxing and ceremonials including the Coronation of 1937. He was thus able to build up time at the microphone which is the best possible way of learning to broadcast.

During the war he was a war correspondent for the BBC and landed in Normandy on D-Day with the invasion forces. I remember hearing his report on the first evening from Broadcasting House in London. He had landed in Normandy early in the morning, and had then been rushed back to Broadcasting House – still in his dirty battledress.

It was some time before he did actual live cricket commentary in the thirties. Like the Football League, the cricket authorities were frightened of the effect it would have on their gates, so it was not until 1938 that he was allowed into the grounds to describe play as it was happening. Before this he used to sit in the Press Box and rush out of the ground at intervals and close of play to broadcast from some nearby building where the BBC engineers had set up their equipment.

In 1934 I heard his reports on the Lord's Test Match against Australia – Hedley Verity's match when he took 15 wickets for 104 runs. The reports must have been good because I can still recall his description of Patsy Hendren's tumbling catch at silly point, where he caught Tim Wall off Verity, and finished the match.

It was during this Test that Howard had to rush to the basement of a borrowed house in nearby Grove End Road to do his reports. For one of them he arrived breathless to find that the young daughter of the house was having a piano lesson upstairs. The first part of his report had a background of scales, until one of the engineers persuaded the young girl to stop. But her mother was not too pleased, and after a minute or so came down and rapped on the window of the basement, shouting, 'How much longer? My little girl's wasting her music lesson!'

Howard was normally quiet and unexcitable, but on one occasion a listener did write in to complain. She said that when McCabe was bowled by Farnes, Howard let out a fearful shout of 'He's out!' and sounded as if he had swallowed his tonsils. She went on, 'The Prince of Broadcasters had raised his voice'!

As you may have gathered, in the days of Sir John Reith (as he was when Director-General) a commentator had to be very careful what he said on the air. Goodness knows what Sir John would have said about some of our goings-on in the *Test Match Special* box today. As an example of what I mean, Howard was once describing the bowling of the Australian, Bill O'Reilly. The Tiger, as he was called, was bowling magnificently and skittling out the England side. So Howard plucked up courage and actually sang over the air:

> If you're the O'Reilly,
> They speak of so highly,
> Gor' Blimey, O'Reilly,
> You *are* bowling well.

It was the Gor' Blimey which did it, and in addition to an internal reprimand, Howard received a lot of letters of rebuke from the listeners. One anonymous writer wrote:

> My dear Slobber-Chops,
> Now you've done it. 'Gor' Blimey' indeed. We know you're not the Archbishop of Canterbury but need you descend to blasphemy? I hope they excommunicate you!

CHAPTER 3

Links in the Chain

After the war, there were several people working on outside broadcasts who had joined the department before the war and who therefore formed a link with the early pioneering years. On the administrative side there was Lobby himself, Michael Standing and Charles Max-Muller. Michael had joined the BBC in 1935 and until 1940 was a commentator and interviewer, and in cricket he often partnered Howard Marshall.

Charles Max-Muller was never a broadcaster but for years before the war was General Manager of O.B.s. After war service he returned to the BBC in the overseas service and then became Head of Outside Broadcasts in 1952, when Lobby went to television. He had tremendous energy and never stood still for a moment, with a habit of jingling the coins in his pocket. There was nothing he did not know about the workings of the BBC and he also knew everyone in it. His contacts outside the BBC were wide and varied and this was of great value to the department in setting up broadcasts and fixing contracts. He was a superb organizer of such big broadcasting operations as the Coronation, Olympic Games and so on. Certainly under his guidance the O.B. Department spread its wings and became an even more important part of the BBC. He was a very keen traveller and there was great rivalry between him and Peter Dimmock in Television as to which of them could clock up the most overseas miles in a year.

On the engineering side, R. H. Wood was Engineer in Charge of O.B.s for just under thirty years, from 1935 to 1964. He was responsible for the vast technical operations involved in all big outside broadcasts, and these included two Coronations, the funerals of King George VI and Sir

Winston Churchill, and three Royal Weddings.

He was a special favourite of King George VI and Queen Elizabeth, and did much to help the King over his difficulties with his stammer. He was regularly 'in attendance' each Christmas for the King's Christmas Broadcast which in those days was done 'live', with the King in his study at Sandringham, and his family all listening in another room. The King – and later our present Queen – always expected R.H. to be there to nurse them through any important broadcast. He had a quiet confidential way of speaking, almost in a whisper, and unintentionally amused the Royal Family – and all of us – with his famous malapropisms. Here are a few examples: 'He ran out of the room like a house on fire'; 'Now he's buttered his bread he must lie on it'; 'He's as happy as a sandbag'; 'He puts his finger into every tart'.

He had a long reign and ran his department with an apparent remoteness and vagueness about what was going on. But of course he *did* know, and rightly had confidence in, all his O.B. engineers, who both as men and technicians were the pick of the engineering staff. They are a vital part of any broadcast, not only for their technical skills, but because they are ambassadors for the BBC wherever they go to set up a broadcast. Commentary has always been a team effort and the friendly cooperation and partnership between commentator and engineer has been one of the strengths of the O.B.s, and has always made this type of broadcast a real pleasure to do.

John Snagge

On the broadcasting side there were two main links between pre-war and post-war O.B.s.

The first of these was John Snagge – possibly the most versatile of all broadcasters, certainly one of the best, and definitely the longest standing. He joined the BBC as Assistant Director of BBC Stoke-on-Trent – a lofty title but he actually had to do all the bits and pieces, including announcing. This was in 1924 and until 1981 he was broadcasting from then on. He became an announcer at Savoy Hill in 1928 in the days when they all had to put on dinner jackets to read the news. They also used to have a pianola in the studio, which the announcer was responsible for playing to fill in occasional interludes. One day John was off duty in the rest room when he heard strangled noises coming from the studio. He rushed in, to find that the tie of one of his colleagues had caught in the pianola roll, and he was gradually being pulled into the pianola and strangled to death. Later on Ernest Lush took over from the pianola and used to play the piano to fill in. Stuart Hibberd – the announcer known as 'Golden Voice' – is reputed to have said, 'There will now be an interlush by Ernest Lude.'

In John's early days at Stoke he was a conspicuous figure in his Oxford Bags, unexpected gear for an old Wykehamist and son of a judge. But when he came to London the standard of dress was higher and if anyone's shoes were down at heel the offender was sent out immediately to get them mended. He will always be famous all over the world for his commentaries on the Oxford and Cambridge Boat Race. He did his first commentary in 1931 and was main commentator on the race for the next fifty years, until he retired in 1980 – and then in 1981 it took *four* commentators to replace him. He has plenty of memories of those fifty years. In 1949 in a desperately close race he made his best-known 'gaffe': '. . . it's a very close race – I can't see who is in the lead – it's either Oxford or Cambridge!'

In 1952 he missed the thrilling Oxford victory by a canvas because his launch broke down, and radio had to take the television commentary for the exciting finish. He once said of an Australian blue: 'He's the only overseas blue rowing in *both* boats!'

John tells one lovely story about the Boat Race. Every year when the boats reached Duke's Meadows on the Middlesex bank there was a man there who ran up the dark and light blue flags on a pole, showing the approximate distances between the crews at that stage. John was normally quite a long way back, so used to look to see which flag was in the ascendancy. He then based his judgement of the crews' positions by the two flags on the pole. Once at some rowing function John met the man who operated the flags. The man did not recognize John, who asked him how he always worked out the correct distances between the boats so accurately. 'Oh,' replied the man, 'I always listen to John Snagge's commentary!'

There are actually not so many stories about the Boat Race. But four years ago, on the day before the race, a lady on the towpath was watching the crews in their final practice. She approached Tom Boswell – one of our commentary team – and said: 'I wonder if you can explain something to me. I come to see the Boat Race every year. How does it happen that the same two crews are always in the final?'

Some people thought that the Boat Race would be no more when John retired in 1980 aged seventy-five. For fifty years his voice had told the world about it and he must have been one of the few people alive who had never heard the Boat Race commentary. His great strength was his complete knowledge of all things to do with rowing. He had known all the world's great oarsmen over the period and knew all the inside talk and gossip. Every year he used to dine with both crews in the last week before the race and presented them with a George IV golden sovereign dated 1829 – the first year of the race – for them to toss with. He was remarkably impartial and never let his Oxonian background influence his commentary, either in the many years when Oxford were generally the losers, nor in the last decade when they have been on top. Unlike so many of us other commentators he never got over-excited and kept his cool even in the most exciting moments.

The Boat Race, Henley Regatta and Olympic Games, which John covered throughout his career, were actually only a small part of his broadcasting life. He joined O.B.s in 1933 and covered almost every sport either as commentator, reporter, or as the 'Square One' man. In addition he did a variety of what can be called stunts in a programme called *Let's Go Somewhere*. (This title was 'pinched' by a certain B. Johnston for his live four-minute spot in *In Town Tonight* 1948–1952.) He also commentated on a number of events such as the Aldershot Tattoo when, on seeing the Royal Car arrive escorted by a military policeman on a motor-bike, he said, 'Here comes Queen Mary and her motor cycle.'

During the war John moved over to become Presentation Director, and in addition to becoming an announcer once again, was in charge of all the others as well. His rich, deep voice, unlike any other, was so easily recognizable that it was ideal for wartime. It gave a feeling of trust, confidence and credibility, and soon earned him the sobriquet of The Voice of London. Perhaps his most famous wartime broadcast was the announcement of the Normandy landings on D-Day. I remember hearing it in Hove where the Guards Armoured Division was waiting with its tanks. But in addition to D-Day he also announced V.E. Day, V.J. Day and the deaths of King George VI and Queen Mary.

His job as Head of Presentation meant that he had little time for commentary but in 1953 he was the radio commentator in Westminister Abbey, against strong opposition from Richard Dimbleby who covered the Coronation on television.

In 1954 he was told by the Director-General: 'Don't make any announcements without my personal permission. Your voice is so associated with important announcements that as soon as you come on, people will assume that Winston Churchill has died.'

His career came full circle when in the last few years before he finally gave up broadcasting in 1980, he did a series for Radio London called *John Snagge's London*. He recorded over a hundred of these in which he met people, tried out their jobs or visited interesting and historic places. It was *Let's Go Somewhere* all over again and he even went down in a diver's suit, rode on a fire-engine to a fire and travelled on the Post Office underground railway. An apt comment might have been: 'Back to SQUARE ONE.'

John is as friendly a person as he sounds, with a fund of BBC stories going right back to 1924 and the days of Sir John Reith. My own favourite, perhaps naturally, is the occasion when he was reading out the cricket scores. He said: 'Yorkshire 232 all out – Hutton ill – I'm sorry. Hutton one hundred and eleven'!

Another one occurred in 1939 when the King and Queen were paying a visit to Canada, crossing the Atlantic in H.M.S. *Vanguard* – John was the commentator at the quayside and the broadcast was scheduled to last for twenty minutes. John had done his homework and while the tugs were fussing around the big ship, he described the scene, the crowds, the Royal Marines Band, the bunting and details of the *Vanguard* and the programme of the tour in Canada. But unfortunately the tugs were having some difficulty and the twenty minutes soon became thirty. John was running out of material from all his notes, so for the umpteenth time said the King and Queen were waving from the bridge. He then noticed that the Queen whispered something to the King and immediately left the bridge: 'Ah,' said John, 'the Queen has now left the bridge and gone below for some reason or other.' He then got stuck for something more to say and after a few seconds added in desperation: '. . . and now I can see water coming through the side of the ship.'

For the record, John was *not* responsible for the following, which was said by an unknown commentator one year at Henley Royal Regatta: 'It's a very close race. Lady Margaret and Jesus are rowing neck and neck. Perhaps Lady Margaret is just ahead . . . but no, Jesus is now definitely making water on Lady Margaret'!

Wynford Vaughan-Thomas

The second main link with the pre-war broadcasters is Wynford Vaughan-Thomas, who in his mid-seventies is still his ebullient and effervescent self and broadcasting regularly for such diverse occasions as the Royal Wedding or riding round Wales on a horse. He is, I would say, the most gifted of all commentators, with a wide variety of talents and immense knowledge of practically everything, as demonstrated in many quiz and general knowledge games. His talents are awe-inspiring. With his Welsh gift of the gab, the words just flow from his mouth with the lilting inflections of a true Welshman. He is a highly entertaining raconteur in the Peter Ustinov class, and his travels abroad both in war and peace have given him a vast supply of material. With a retentive memory, a sense of humour and the ability and wit to gild the lily he makes the most of his material and can keep a roomful of people spellbound for hours. He is a musician and still plays the piano like a professional. He is a draughtsman who can illustrate his own writings and he is a connoisseur of wines and food in almost every country in the world. His knowledge of history and geography would shame any schoolmaster. A remarkable, rather small, grey-haired, rotund man who in spite of a penchant for good living keeps himself so fit that he is still enjoying his chief hobby – climbing mountains.

As a commentator he has an encyclopedic vocabulary and the gift of description, and is really the last of the old-fashioned 'Lobby men'. He joined the BBC in 1934 and since commentating on King George VI's Coronation, has performed at all subsequent major events, including royal tours. His bubbling enthusiasm brings every occasion to life, and if it may sometimes run away with him, it enables him to portray everything in a better light. With Wynford there is no such thing as a boring broadcast.

He was one of the BBC's star war correspondents, and made an epic recording in a bomber flying over Berlin during an air-raid in 1941. He covered the Anzio landings in Italy and whether by intent or mistake was the first ashore from his particular landing-craft. There followed his hilarious adventures with the Americans both in Italy and the south of France, and finally the crossing of the Rhine. This ended with his famous broadcast from the desk of Lord Haw-Haw in Hamburg, on which were an empty gin bottle and a copy of his last script, left by the fleeing traitor. A most satisfying climax to a war correspondent's wartime service to be able to broadcast through Lord Haw-Haw's actual microphone using those chilling words we had heard so often during the last five years: 'Geermany Calling. Geermany Calling' – even though there was the suspicion of a Welsh accent.

It was Wynford who gave me my test when I was being considered for a job in O.B.s at the end of 1945. He was doing interviews one Saturday night outside the Monseigneur Newsreel Theatre at Marble Arch. When he had finished his programme he gave me a short lesson in the art of interviewing. Get to 'know' the person you are about to interview and gain their confidence – if you have the time. Never ask a question to which the person can only answer yes or no. Although always having a next question ready, listen to the answer to your last one; there may be a completely different question to ask as a result of that answer. Be courteous, friendly, don't hector. But if the answer is evasive or inconclusive, press on politely until you get something definite. And finally – and most important – remember you are only the link between the listeners and the person being interviewed. They want to hear him or her, so keep your own opinions to yourself, your questions as short as possible, and don't swamp your victim with your own personality.

This was excellent advice of which many modern interviewers might well take heed. Anyhow, when Wynford had finished I recorded my interviews with passers-by, asking them what they thought of the butter ration. Well, if you ask silly questions ... But although I wasn't very good, Wynford reported to Lobby that at least I kept talking and did not dry up. So I'm afraid you have to blame Wynford if you have been listening to me for the last thirty-seven years.

Wynford, as you can imagine, has hundreds of stories – both serious and comic – about his many broadcasts and travels. It would be invidious to 'pinch' his material, though in writing it could never be as good as when told by Wynford. However as one so prone to 'gaffes' myself I cannot resist retelling a couple of stories.

Wynford was once the commentator at a television outside broadcast from a steel works. The idea was to demonstrate how automation and new techniques had increased efficiency in production. As a white-hot rod of steel passed him along a conveyor belt Wynford shouted above the din of the works, 'Here comes thirty foot of white-hot steel, *untouched by human hand*'!

His most famous mistake happened when he was the commentator for television at the launching of the *Ark Royal* at Birkenhead by the Queen Mother. The producer, Ray Lakeland, had told Wynford beforehand: 'Don't talk while the Queen Mother is breaking the bottle of champagne on the bows of the ship. Keep quiet as the *Ark Royal* glides slowly down the slipway. Wait until she actually hits the water and then start talking to your heart's content.'

All went according to plan. Number one camera showed the Queen Mother making her short speech and breaking the bottle. Number two camera showed the ship as it gradually moved, and number three had shots of the cheering crowd. Ray punched all these up in turn so that they came on to the screens of the viewers at home. Then just before the *Ark Royal* reached the water he noticed number one camera had got a marvellous picture of the Queen Mother smiling in that charming way she has. Ray was so enchanted that he forgot all that he had told Wynford and immediately pressed the button which filled the viewers' screens with the Queen Mother: this unfortunately coincided with the exact moment that the *Ark Royal* hit the water. Wynford was watching this and not his television screen, and remembering his instructions began to talk: 'There she is,' he said, 'the huge vast bulk of her!'

Harold Abrahams

Another, less obvious, link was Harold Abrahams, the only broadcaster whom I knew who had a film made about him – that splendid British picture *Chariots of Fire*. He was a Cambridge athletics blue and won a gold medal in the one hundred metres in the Olympic Games at Paris in 1924. Before the war he was used mostly as a commentator but from 1945 was more often the expert-comments-man, keeper of records, and unofficial time-keeper, with Rex Alston doing the commentary. That time-keeping was absolutely vital to him. Wherever he went he was armed with at least three stopwatches. I swear that when one was speaking to him he would often time the conversation. Although it was a fetish with him, the reports on lap-times in a race were of tremendous help to the commentators in building up the interest and excitement.

Harold himself occasionally showed bias in his commentary. In the 1936 Olympic Games in Berlin he was commentating on the 1,500 metres. Jack Lovelock, the New

Zealander, was a personal friend of Harold, and he could not suppress his pride in the Empire when he saw that Lovelock was going to win: 'Jack, Jack, come on Jack,' he cried. 'He's done it, my God he's done it! Lovelock, Lovelock, Lovelock!'

In those pre-war years he was always formally attired and in 1927 at the Varsity Sports there is a picture of him wearing his black Homburg hat whilst talking into the microphone. He was one of the few experts in the early days who was prepared to find the time to analyse and discuss his broadcasts, in spite of his busy life as a civil servant and athletics administrator. He formed a splendid team with his old friend Rex Alston who had been his number two in the sprints. Harold had a dry sense of humour and a quick wit. In 1955 he was describing the finish of the Windsor to Chiswick marathon. By mistake he did not notice the leading runner McMinnis enter the stadium, and wrongly gave the winner as Iden, who was actually second. When his mistake was pointed out to him, he quickly apologized, claiming it was a case of mistaken IDENtity.

Right up to the end Harold took tremendous trouble with his broadcasts and attended all the meetings before and after a big event. Even though his knowledge of everything to do with athletics was better than anyone else's, he was still willing to learn.

He once showed me a little booklet which he had produced. It was typical of his love of detail and must have involved much journeying to and fro on the Underground. The booklet showed where all the WAY OUT signs were situated on every London Tube Station, and the number of the carriage which always stopped exactly opposite the exit. For instance, if you were travelling from St John's Wood to Oxford Circus you would need to travel in the third coach. But for Charing Cross it would be the first one. I don't know about you but I always seem to get into the wrong end of the train, and would dearly love to have a copy of Harold's *Guide to the Exits*.

Part Two Familiar Voices

CHAPTER 4

My Start at the BBC

It was with some trepidation that I reported to No. 55 Portland Place early in January 1946. This was the temporary home of the Outside Broadcasts Department, presided over by Lobby in what was once – and is again today – a luxurious four- or five-bedroom flat. For the sixth time in my life I was to be a new boy – preparatory school, Eton, Freshman at Oxford – the family business – the Grenadiers – and now the BBC. But my fears were groundless. Although Lobby, Stewart Macpherson and Wynford were the only people I knew, I was received in a most friendly way and was soon made 'one of the family'. As I was soon to find out, there *was* a tremendous family spirit in the department, and a sense of unity and pride. There were two main reasons for this – Lobby's leadership and the fact that we were on our own at No. 55, away from the managerial and administrative atmosphere of Broadcasting House. Although most of the famous commentators left the staff and went freelance soon after I arrived, I was never tempted to do so. I have always enjoyed working closely with other people, and I found complete happiness in remaining loyal to O.B.s.

Anyway, as it was a Monday I was immediately plunged into the weekly departmental meeting, and I was surprised by what I saw. There, sitting humbly with notebooks in hand were well-known commentators like Raymond Glendenning, Rex Alston, Wynford Vaughan-Thomas and Stewart Macpherson. They listened quietly while Lobby criticized, praised, or completely pulled to bits the programmes which they had broadcast during the previous week. This was the strength of the department. No one was too big to escape a masterly analysis of their broadcasts.

How Lobby managed it, I don't know, but he tried to listen to all the output of O.B.s, and record his findings into a little black book. He was a perfectionist, but completely fair, never too fulsome with his praise but never too unkind either: 'Not bad,' or 'On the whole a brave effort,' meant that you had done pretty well. But if he began to beat his clenched right hand into the palm of his left and say, 'Brian, I was a bit puzzled . . .' you could be sure that you were about to be criticized. But no one resented this because the criticism was always constructive.

For as long as Lobby was Head of O.B.s, most of us used to telephone him at his home immediately after a broadcast, and ask anxiously for his verdict. It was quite a tense moment as one wanted to hear if that fist would start beating, something he seemed able to do whilst holding a telephone receiver in his hand. When he left for television this habit of telephoning after each broadcast gradually died out. The weekly meetings still take place today but deal more with administrative affairs than the quality of broadcasting.

One of the troubles is that the sports output of O.B.s has increased so much that it is practically impossible for one man to monitor each programme. This is a great pity because undoubtedly the knowledge that a friendly Big Brother was listening not only kept everyone on their toes, but also prevented them getting into bad habits with their speech or descriptions.

I know, for instance, that over the last twenty years I have made many mistakes but honestly cannot remember any of the Heads of O.B.s telling me about them. I am sure they would claim, as I have suggested, that they don't have the time to listen to and analyse all the output. Some, too, have been administrators pure and simple, and may have felt unqualified to offer advice to established broadcasters. But this does mean that a young man starting as a commentator can get into bad habits or do or say wrong things, blissfully ignorant that he is doing so. Whether the standards have dropped is not for me to say, but with less direction from the top a new boy must find it that much harder to perfect his technique.

I have been tremendously lucky all my life and once again

I fell on my feet on joining O.B.s. I was allotted to John Ellison as his assistant. He was responsible for the live broadcasts from West End musicals, music halls and seaside concert parties. I had always loved the theatre and am really a frustrated actor, who overcomes this by after-dinner speaking. Ever since leaving school I had haunted all the music halls in London. So you can understand how pleased I was that, under John's tuition, I was able to learn the art of live commentary from a theatre. We would choose a half-hour excerpt from a musical and it was then one's job to sit in a box and act as the eyes of the listener, by describing the non-musical parts. In this way the listener could visualize the scenery, costumes and action on the stage. It was an admirable way to learn because it was necessary to be slick and economical in words, and to time one's comments so as not to clash with the music and singing, which the listener would want to hear uninterrupted. John was an ideal person to teach me as he himself had been an actor, and knew almost everyone in the theatrical world. This was a wonderful bonus for me as I got to know all the stars of musical comedy and the music hall, some of them, like Harry Secombe, Max Bygraves, Peter Sellers and Frankie Howerd, new boys like myself.

But though in the first few months I was to do a lot of these showbiz broadcasts, my very first commentary came from an unlikely place – one of the ladies' lavatories in St James's Park. In February 1946 an unexploded bomb was discovered at the bottom of the lake, which was then drained, so that the sappers could blow up the bomb. The BBC decided to interrupt programmes for this dramatic event, and Lobby thought it would be a good opportunity for my first 'live' broadcast. He went to the park with me, and we took up our position on a small bridge. But a policeman told us it was too exposed and suggested that we went inside the nearby lavatory. By standing on one of the seats I was able to give my commentary, looking out through those louvre-type windows. I was naturally very nervous, but managed to describe the explosion and its after-effects. But I got so excited that at the end I promised listeners a bigger and better bomb the following week! I always add that I came out of the loo looking a bit flushed!

In March my lucky streak continued. My telephone rang and it was Ian Orr-Ewing, just out of the RAF and now Head of Television Outside Broadcasts. He and I had played a lot of cricket together before the war, and he knew how much I loved it, and that I knew something about it. He explained that television was starting up again after its wartime lay-off and that they wanted to televise the two London Test Matches against India, and would I like to have a shot at doing the commentary? You can guess my answer and as a result of that lucky friendship with Ian I was to be one of the television cricket commentators for the next twenty-four years.

There had only been four Tests televised before the war, two in 1938 and two in 1939, all from Lord's and the Oval. There was therefore no one who knew about the techniques of television commentary and we had to learn as we went along, at the expense of the poor viewers; though fortunately, perhaps, there were not too many of them in those early days.

Lobby had laid down the basic principles of radio commentary with his Pyramid Method. But no one seemed to have attempted the same thing for television, and we had to try to work it out ourselves. The only advice we were given was: 'Never speak unless you can add to the picture.' This is basically sound advice, but easier said than done. There is no doubt in my mind that television commentary is far more difficult than radio. I have always maintained that a TV commentator can never please *everybody* even *some* of the time. He will in fact be jolly lucky to please *anybody all* the time. If he talks too much the well-informed viewers will say, 'Why can't he put a sock in it?' But if he talks too little other viewers who don't know much about the game or ceremony will complain, 'Why can't he give us more details and explain what is going on?' The ideal television commentator should be just like a knowledgeable friend who goes to the match or ceremony with you. This friend does not point out the things you can obviously see, but dots the 'i's and helps you understand what is going on by identifying people, by explaining the laws or regulations of a game,

or the details of a procession or ceremony. But he must still
be careful not to describe the obvious. In an old edition of
Punch a television commentator (probably me) was accused
of saying, 'Now there's a picture which tells its own tale' –
and then proceeding to describe it in detail.

I think that most people nowadays realize that a TV
commentator has to put up with what we call 'dirty talk-
back'. This means that while he is commentating he will be
receiving instructions from his producer through his headphones. Or even worse, he will hear the producer talking to
his four or five cameramen, giving them their instructions
while the poor commentator tries to concentrate on what he
is describing. This is not easy and certainly took a lot of
getting used to in the early days. He has to remember *not* to
answer the producer back.

For instance, if the producer says, 'Give the score,' it is
very tempting to answer, as R.C. Robertson-Glasgow once
did, 'For those who weren't listening when I gave the score
just now, it is . . .' Or like Percy Fender, who when told to
stick to the play and not reminisce about his old Surrey
days, turned to me, luckily with his hand over the microphone, and said, 'If he's so damn clever, why doesn't he
come up here and do the commentary himself?'

But the real art of television commentary is to know when
and when not to speak, and to make sure that when you do,
your remark is short, concise and matches the picture. Short
and concise because although there should be close cooperation between the producer and commentator, the picture can suddenly change to something else and make a
nonsense of what the commentator is saying. It is this need
for the neat, precise comment that makes television so much
more difficult than radio. A gaffe, a joke which falls flat, or
an inaccurate statement stands out like a sore thumb on
television. In the continuous talk of radio commentary these
mistakes are often camouflaged by the flow of speech.

And so I set out to learn the craft of commentary on both
radio and television. And doing the same thing were many
other commentators who have become household names
today.

*

1948 was another lucky year for me. I got engaged to and married my wife Pauline. The Australians were touring England and it was the first time I had ever commentated on an England *v* Australia Test Match. I also started a new series called 'Let's Go Somewhere' as part of the popular and well-established *In Town Tonight*.

For some years there had been a live outside broadcast spot in the programme, which was broadcast every Saturday night. It started with Michael Standing's 'Standing on the Corner', and then became 'Man in the Street' with Stewart Macpherson and Harold Warrender as the interviewers.

My colleague in O.B.s, John Ellison, took over from them and changed the spot to 'On the Job', in which he visited people who were working on Saturday night. One Saturday in March he was to interview an air hostess in a BOAC plane during its flight from Prestwick to London. In case the ground-to-air contact failed, he asked me to stand by with another air hostess at London Airport. Once again I was lucky. The engineers could not contact John in the plane, so I did my interview on the ground instead.

A few weeks later, John took over the more important job as interviewer in the studio, and the producer, Peter Duncan, asked me to continue with 'On the Job'. Except for my honeymoon I did it through the spring and early summer, but somehow it did not seem to amount to very much. It was all talk and too similar to what was taking place in the studio. So Peter Duncan asked Lobby and me whether we could not do something with movement, excitement or humour in complete contrast to the scripted interviews of *In Town Tonight*. We decided to revive the feature called 'Let's Go Somewhere' which John Snagge had done in the thirties, and we broadcast the first one in October. For the next four years on every Saturday night when *In Town Tonight* was on the air (they took an annual summer holiday) I went 'somewhere', until after one hundred and fifty I thought that I had done enough.

It turned out to be one of the luckiest breaks of my whole career. *In Town Tonight*, in those days before the spread of television, was one of the BBC's top programmes, and was listened to by millions of people. This meant that I began to become fairly well known as a broadcaster. But even more important, it was the best possible school for broadcasting. I learnt more about the techniques of commentary and the use of the microphone than I could ever have done by any other means.

The point was that each broadcast was 'live', lasted about four minutes and was never recorded. This meant that each Saturday was a 'first night', and I either got it right or wrong. There could be no retakes. As a result we had our failures, but I hope some successes too. But it was inevitably hit or miss. I had no producer to help me, and even had to carry – and keep an eye on – a stopwatch. There was just myself and my faithful engineer, Nogs Newman, who with occasional relief from Oggie Lomas, gave up all his Saturday nights to be with me.

It really was a great chance to practise the arts of commentary, exact timing, description and correct use of the microphone. This is something unfortunately denied the modern up-and-coming commentator. How can he acquire the confidence which these one hundred and fifty broadcasts gave to me? There are just not the opportunities these days. The microphone really became part of me, and no matter what I was doing I soon began to forget it was there.

The variety of things which I covered also sharpened my commentary technique and improved my powers of description, whilst the conditions under which I often had to broadcast taught me never to expect too much comfort, or protection from the weather. Here is a list of some of the things I did in 'Let's Go Somewhere':

Staying alone in the Chamber of Horrors
Riding a horse bare-back at a circus
Riding on a motor-bike through a wall of barrels
Lying under a passing train
Being hauled out of the sea by helicopter
Being shaved and shampooed by the Crazy Gang on
    the stage of the Victoria Palace during a show
Singing in the street disguised as a tramp
Being attacked by a police dog

Being shot out of an ejection seat
Going down a coal mine
Being hypnotized
Riding on a fire-engine to a fire
Being sawn in half
Being a bird in a Flying Ballet in an ice pantomime
Playing a cinema organ
Singing 'Underneath the Arches' with Bud Flanagan
    outside the Victoria Palace
Broadcasting from inside a letter box (at the end of
    this I put my hand out through the slot to take a
    letter, and the lady posting it fainted!)

I hope that these examples are sufficient to show what a wonderful schooling it all was, and how lucky I was to have had the opportunity to commentate under such difficult and varied conditions!

CHAPTER 5

Now Over To . . .

Freddy Grisewood

When I joined Outside Broadcasts there were two famous names attached to them. Freddy Grisewood had an office in 55 Portland Place and whilst rationing was still on continued his wartime programmes on food, catering and cooking. He also did the television commentary on the Coronation procession in 1937 and the Victory Parade in 1946. He was a fine games player at both cricket and lawn tennis and until Dan Maskell took over in 1951 he was the main television commentator at Wimbledon. Like so many athletes he later became riddled with arthritis, and restricted his activities to the programme which made him one of the best known voices, and best loved broadcasters on radio. This was of course *Any Questions?* which is still going as strong as ever today. Freddy was its very first chairman when it was originally broadcast on 12 October 1948. Freddy was a loveable man with a crinkly face and was a fine singer of songs in a rich Gloucestershire dialect. His particularly friendly style suited television perfectly but I never remember him doing a radio commentary.

Gilbert Harding

The other famous person – and a considerable one! – with O.B.s was Gilbert Harding. He joined them in 1940 after a varied career. He studied for orders in the Church of England but later became a Roman Catholic. He had been a schoolmaster, lecturer and policeman and at one time was the *Times* correspondent in Cyprus. No one can recollect his doing an actual commentary but he used to take part in wartime programmes with Wynford Vaughan-Thomas and Stewart Macpherson. Most people will remember Gilbert as the testy, intolerant and impatient panellist in *What's My Line?* He was all of these things but had a fine brain and could not tolerate inefficiency of any sort, either by a waiter in a restaurant or an official in, for example, the railways or Post Office. There was an excuse for this impatience and 'won't stand fools at any price' attitude. He was for most of his life a sick man, with several complaints too numerous to mention. But he was usually contrite the day following the many incidents in which he became involved either on television, radio or in his personal life.

His manner and his character were not ideal for the job of interviewer which he performed with Wynford and Stewart. In one programme, in a country town somewhere, they were stopping people in the street and asking them what they did. An obvious countryman approached Gilbert, who stopped him and asked him tersely and gruffly, 'What are you?' The man somewhat naturally resented this aggressive approach and replied, 'What's that got to do with you?'

'I'm from the BBC,' said Gilbert sharply.

'Oh, well then,' said the man reluctantly. 'I suppose I'd better tell you. I'm a gentleman farmer.'

'Impossible!' said Gilbert with a snort. 'You can't be both!'

Gilbert once told me what is one of my favourite cricket stories. As a boy at school he was fat and short-sighted and quite hopeless at cricket. So much so that his headmaster finally gave in, and told Gilbert that instead of playing cricket he should go for walks. This infuriated the young cricket master, who thought he would get his own back on Gilbert. When he put the names on the board for the players in the School *v* Masters match, underneath he wrote: 'Umpire – G. Harding.'

The Masters batted first and the young cricket master hit the boys' bowling all over the field. He had soon reached 95 not out when the boy bowling from Gilbert's end hit him high up on the chest. The boy stifled his appeal for LBW, but not before Gilbert had raised his finger and given the master out. The latter was – perhaps justifiably – furious and as he passed Gilbert on his way back to the pavilion spat out the words, 'Harding, you weren't paying attention. I wasn't out.'

Gilbert reflected for a few seconds and then came back with the memorable reply, 'On the contrary, sir, I *was* paying attention, and you weren't out.'

A sad, complex character, Gilbert, but I got to know him well towards the end of his life and know how much he regretted having been rude to so many people.

Stewart Macpherson

I personally owe a great deal to Stewart. It was through meeting him both during and immediately after the war, that I got the chance to do my test for the BBC at the end of 1945. Although it was not very good, it was sufficient to gain me an interview with Lobby. After much heart searching, I am sure, Lobby took the plunge and offered me a job in the Outside Broadcasts Department. Although he guaranteed neither permanency nor much money, I accepted.

So *I* owed everything to luck. But Stewart owed *his* own job in the BBC to a mixture of cheek and persistence, and, of course, to a large amount of ability. He came over from Canada in 1937 with some sort of introduction to John Snagge – already a broadcasting name well known to listeners overseas. Stewart had done ice hockey commentaries in Canada and had heard that another Canadian ice hockey commentator – Bob Bowman – was switching jobs at the BBC. So Stewart just turned up at Broadcasting House and asked to see John Snagge. John was very busy and sent down a message to reception to say that he was sorry but he could not see Stewart that day. Three hours later he went down in the lift to go to lunch, and saw waiting at reception a short, bespectacled man with a large head. It was Stewart, who somehow recognized John, waylaid him, and persuaded him to ask the BBC to give him a test.

The BBC were looking rather desperately for someone to replace Bowman and they quickly organized a board of high-up officials to try out Stewart in Broadcasting House.

They obviously could not produce an ice hockey match, so asked Stewart to sit in a studio and give an imaginary commentary. The board sat in the control room, and gave him the signal to start. For most people it would have been an impossible task to make up the names of players and describe the run of play and the score in a game which was not taking place. But Stewart took it in his stride and went off at a tremendous pace, giving a very exciting commentary packed with action, fouls and goals. After about five minutes he stopped, thinking he had done enough. The panel were visibly impressed. In fact he had made it so realistic that one of the board asked him to continue the commentary, as he wanted to know the final score!

He was, of course, taken on and became the ice hockey commentator. Then when war was declared he did a number of broadcasts for O.B.s before becoming a distinguished BBC war correspondent.

After the war he was the number one boxing and ice hockey commentator. He was ideally suited for both, with his quick-fire delivery and racy style of description, spiced with a number of transatlantic expressions new to British listeners. He was certainly in the top three of fast talkers, with another Canadian called Gerry Wilmot and Raymond Glendenning as his rivals. He became famous for his close harmony with W. Barrington Dalby, signalling the end of each round with a crisp invitation to 'Come on in, Barry.'

In addition to commentary Stewart also made his name – and good money! – by being chairman of *Twenty Questions* and *Ignorance is Bliss*. In late 1946 and early 1947 he had also tried his hand as the first presenter of *Down Your Way*, which started only in London. There was no preliminary research as there is today. Then, *Down Your Way* just selected a street or a district and with a list of house occupiers knocked haphazardly on doors. On his twelfth programme Stewart did this once too often. After he had knocked on one door, a large man appeared and Stewart, looking down at his list of names, said, 'Good morning, sir. Is Mrs Brown in?' 'Oh,' said the large man, 'you're the chap who's been after my missis, are you?' – and proceeded to slug Stewart a nasty blow. Hasty retreat of the *Down Your*

Way party and the last programme which Stewart did. He found the calm and peace of boxing and ice hockey safer!

It was a great loss to British radio when early in the 1950s he decided for family reasons to return to his native Canada. He would have made a big impact too on television and – funnily for such a naturally fast talker – would surely have made a hit on one of the slowest of all sports, golf, which was his favourite hobby.

He was always ready to help with advice and encouragement and I picked up many tips just by watching him at work. One of these can be especially helpful for a commentator at a big state occasion or procession, or even more so at a firework display, which was where I saw Stewart doing it.

He merely had a blank pad of paper in front of him and wrote on it all the adjectives he thought he might need during the display: brilliant – fantastic – magnificent – sparkling – beautiful – colourful – and so on. Then during the broadcast he carefully crossed off each adjective as he used it, and so avoided any repetition. It sounds simple and perhaps unexpected from such a great natural broadcaster. But it is the end result which counts and he certainly nearly always achieved the best.

By the way, we all have to fight against repetition. We often find ourselves plagued by the same adjective coming out of our mouth, time and time again. I wonder if any of you have noticed that my particular *bête noire* is 'marvellous'.

Lionel Marson

I admit that I am fairly emotional and that there have been quite a few occasions on the air when I have found it difficult to speak because of a lump in my throat. But there is only one commentator whom I have actually seen cry with tears running down his cheeks. They were tears of happiness for a great victory by a combination of man and beast. The occasion was the White City in 1951 when Foxhunter – ridden and owned by Harry Llewellyn – won the King George V Cup for the third time.

I had somehow got involved in doing commentary on show jumping. I had few qualifications except that as a rather terrified young boy I used to hunt, and later up at Oxford rode once in a point-to-point or 'grind' as they are called there. I hired a horse called Tip Top who was a half-brother of Tom Walls's Derby winner, April the 5th. The horse did not know it but he could have stopped when he liked. However, his racing instinct prevailed and although left at the start we completed the course and finished fifth. Looking back, it was a crazy thing to have done because I took Tip Top's jumping form on trust and never once went over a jump on him before the race. A famous Oxford tipster called Captain Dean summed up my riding perfectly: 'There are jockeys here today who could not ride in a railway carriage unless the door was locked,' he told the crowd!

Anyhow, it was considered enough for me to share the commentary on the International Horse Show with a real expert, ex-cavalry officer and BBC announcer, Lionel Marson. There he was in brown bowler hat and gaiters sitting alongside me. As Foxhunter completed the clear round which made him winner for the third time, Lionel rose, shouting into the microphone and quite openly sobbing his heart out. He was actually in good company as everyone in the stand around us seemed to be doing the same thing.

Lionel was one of the old school, had perfect manners, wore all the right cricket ties and was in fact a 'proper gentleman'. He made one famous boob on the air when reading the news about the theft of the Stone of Scone from Westminster Abbey. The script read: '. . . it had been placed in the Abbey by Edward Ist.' For some reason Lionel pronounced this as Edward *isst*. The duty editor sitting alongside him pointed frantically at the Ist and Lionel, after a second's thought, said, 'I am sorry. I evidently got that wrong. I should of course have said, "Edward *iced*".'

Incidentally, those few show jumping commentaries were the only ones in any sport other than cricket which I have done, with the exception of the Boat Race. Having played a lot of rugby at Eton and Oxford I would like to have had a shot at that, but Rex Alston was firmly in the saddle and I was never given the opportunity. But surprisingly I *was* given a test on soccer early in 1946, when the BBC were short of support commentators for Raymond Glendenning.

Another member of O.B.s, Geoffrey Peck, and I were sent to a mid-week game at Loftus Road. We noticed that on the previous Saturday the Queen's Park Rangers centre-forward McGibbon had scored three goals. The sporting pages headlined him as 'Three Goal McGibbon'. So when I started my test commentary I picked out the number 9 at centre-forward and gave him the full treatment: 'There goes McGibbon – I would recognize his style anywhere – long raking stride, good with his head and a power-driving left foot . . .' and so on. I thought it had all gone rather well. But imagine my horror when I bought an evening paper on the way home and read that McGibbon had been delayed in heavy traffic and had been substituted by another player in the number 9 shirt at the last moment. Lobby rightly thought that I was *not* the man he was looking for.

Raymond Glendenning

In the thirties Teddy Wakelam was the first of the multi-sport commentators with his rugby, soccer, tennis and cricket. The war produced two more, Raymond Glendenning and Rex Alston.

Raymond came to London from the BBC in Northern Ireland in the early 1940s and found the world of sport wide open to his talents. Because of shortage of staff he took on anything and by the end of the war numbered racing, soccer, boxing and tennis as his top sports. Because of Rex he did not do athletics, but was used in the 1948 Olympic Games for the show jumping, and also covered the Greyhound Derby and other races. In fact he was once strictly timed at 176 words in thirty seconds during one race, and over 300 words in a full minute.

So as you can gather he was nothing if not versatile. He had a rich, plummy, mellow voice and had remarkable powers of description. He could describe anything, even our exit from the church when my wife and I were married, and O.B.s gave us a recording of the ceremony. He had a wonderful memory for facts and figures on any sport but of course he never could devote enough time to any one of them. As a result the boxing public were apt to think that he knew more about racing; or the soccer world thought he should concentrate on boxing. It is in fact an impossible task to be the number one expert on such a diversity of sports. For instance, to be a racing commentator you must live racing, go to all the meetings, get to know all the racing personalities well. But Raymond could not do this, so had what was called a 'race-reader' who would stand alongside him feeding him with facts and the position of the horses during the race. This was made possible by the invention of the 'lip-mike', which the commentator held right up to his mouth so that nothing except his voice could be heard by the listener. But you can imagine how difficult it made his job, trying to speak and listen at the same time. The race-readers were full-time racing journalists and one of these was Claude Harrison, followed for a short time by Peter O'Sullevan. The BBC did not try to hide what they were doing, and the race-reader was given his credit over the air.

In boxing Raymond had the help of W. Barrington Dalby – an ex-referee who knew the sport backwards. He summed up for fifty seconds or so between the rounds, but then of course Raymond was left on his own to describe the actual fighting. There was a tremendous furore when Raymond was accused of favouring and shouting home Sugar Ray Robinson in the fight which was in fact won in the end by Randolph Turpin.

Raymond was an easily distinguishable and much caricatured figure. With his horn-rimmed spectacles, his handlebar moustache and his somewhat ample figure he looked in fact not unlike Billy Bunter with a moustache. He was a gregarious person, a great mixer, and greeted by everyone wherever he went. He enjoyed his drink and would recommend a swig of honey in whisky to maintain stamina and the voice during a broadcast. He could speak at a remarkable speed and his voice at the end of a race, or when a goal was scored, reached an incredible crescendo.

It was lucky that he was a good improviser and a bit of an

actor, because on several occasions during the war, he had to commentate on games or races which he could not see. The point was that the BBC was monitored by the Germans, and so no commentator could ever mention anything about the weather. For the same reason no broadcast could ever be cancelled because of fog. When the game or race itself was cancelled because of bad ground conditions, then no commentary took place. There was no explanation to the listener of why not – except perhaps that famous 'technical hitch'.

Certainly on one occasion at Cheltenham Raymond had to invent what was happening while the horses were 'out in the country', only picking them up as they came through the fog in the home straight. Luckily it was not television and he was able to readjust the position of the horses, having been careful to avoid any falls during his fictitious account. There was also fog at Elland Road on Boxing Day 1942, so. Raymond could only see one side of the pitch, and had to make up what was happening on the other side to coincide with the reactions of the crowd on that side. Not easy!

Raymond's silver tongue let him down seriously only once when during the Grand National he remarked, '. . . and now coming to the rider jump there's a waterless horse out in front!'

Raymond gradually faded away in the sixties but for twenty years he had been the BBC's outstanding personality among the sports commentators and the big sporting events were never quite the same without that ample figure with the glasses and handlebar moustache.

Richard Dimbleby

In the sixty years of broadcasting one person stands out head and shoulders above all the rest – that supreme broadcaster Richard Dimbleby. That is a sweeping statement and perhaps can only be truly appreciated by those who were watching television in the fifties and early sixties. For nearly twenty years Richard was the voice of the nation, much loved and respected by every class of listener and viewer. He was arguably the best-known face in Britain and when he died at the early age of fifty-two in December 1965, both the BBC and ITV interrupted programmes to announce his death – ITV beating the BBC to it!

During the closing stages of his long illness he received thousands of cards and letters. Presents poured into St Thomas's Hospital, including six bottles of champagne sent personally by the Queen. The Dean of Westminster offered the Abbey for his memorial service, and it was packed with a congregation of V.I.P.s, his colleagues and friends, and hundreds of ordinary people who had never known him personally. The Queen and Queen Mother were both represented and remarkably the service was televised live by the BBC. I can't imagine the BBC honouring a commentator in such a way today! It only proved what a great influence for good he had been throughout the country. On so many occasions he had related for the ordinary man in the street the things he wanted to hear about the Monarchy and the Country. He was sometimes unkindly accused of being obsequious to the Monarchy and too Establishment-minded. Because he was so often broadcasting on important occasions some people who did not know him also thought that he was pompous. He was unashamedly a royalist and a patriot and had high principles about good manners. This all probably came across in his commentaries. But pompous, never! He had an impish sense of humour with a distinctive chuckle, and could always see the funny side of things. I once went with him as co-driver to report the Monte Carlo Rally and we enjoyed a full ten days of fun and laughter.

He was large, fat and jolly and a wonderful mixer with everyone whom he met, or with whom he worked. O.B. engineers are the best judges of a commentator's character. They work with him at close quarters and see him under strain when things go wrong. They share the triumphs and disasters. I never heard a single word against Richard from any of the television or radio engineers. When he died it seemed like a personal loss to thousands who had never known him other than through his broadcasts. For them the BBC would never be the same again. Nor, in a way, was it.

He began, like so many broadcasters, as a journalist. In

1936, aged twenty-three, he joined the BBC as their *first* news observer. His very first commentary was from Heston Aerodrome, when he described Neville Chamberlain's return from Munich, and we heard Chamberlain's famous 'Out of this nettle danger, we pluck this flower safety.' Three years later, when war broke out, he became the BBC's *first* war correspondent. He came into prominence with his reports from the Middle East desert war. Then when the second front started in Europe he broadcast from anywhere the action took him. From the beaches on D-Day, from Belsen with the first broadcast account of its horrors and from Hitler's armchair in the Chancellery, where he was the first Allied reporter to see the terrible bomb damage. The memory of Belsen was to live with him for the rest of his life.

Back home after the war he became disillusioned with the BBC administrators, who he thought did not fully appreciate his wartime broadcasts. So he resigned from the staff and became a freelance. First of all he was to continue to make his name on radio with programmes like *Down Your Way* (he presented three hundred) and *Twenty Questions*. But television was gradually awakening from its enforced wartime sleep and Richard began to devote most of his time to it. Programmes like *Panorama* made him a well-known face, while his voice – rather like Terry Wogan's today – was in constant demand for every type of commentary, other than sport: King George VI's funeral, the Coronation, royal visits overseas, Princess Margaret's wedding, Trooping the Colour, openings of Parliament, the first cross-Channel television broadcast, Churchill's funeral and a lot more.

His voice was quiet and friendly and I never heard it raised in excitement. He had a superb command of English and always seemed to say the right thing. In fact he had such command of the language and such a quick mind to match it, that his producer on so many royal occasions and other big events, Antony Craxton, has said that he never once heard Richard say 'er'. There are not many of us who could boast that! His timing and his judgement of when to speak or keep quiet on television was impeccable. Television does not require 'waffle'. It needs short, crisp sentences to match the picture. But no matter how perfect the delivery, and the composition of the sentences, the success of a commentator also depends on his material and the information which he is able to give.

This was one of Richard's great strengths. More than almost anyone else at the time – or since – he devoted hours to intense research and preparation before any broadcast. He knew that to sound authoritative he had to know all the facts, and he made sure that he did. He used a number of small white cards with everything he might need to know neatly typed on them in note form. By the end of a broadcast he might not have used more than ten or twenty per cent of them. But they were there – just in case. At Princess Margaret's wedding, when she was nearly an hour late arriving at Tower Bridge to leave for her honeymoon on the royal yacht, no one would have known that anything was wrong. From the notes which he had prepared Richard was able to give the viewer a potted history of the Tower, the River Thames, Tower Bridge, the wharfs, the River Police and the royal yacht itself. He must have been relieved when at last Princess Margaret and Anthony Armstrong-Jones came into sight, but he did not show it.

His professionalism was further illustrated to me the other day by BBC radio producer Geoff Dobson, who as a young trainee worked with Richard on D-Day. Richard had crossed over to Normandy with the invasion forces, and in the evening had been flown back to Dunsfold Aerodrome in Surrey, armed with a number of discs (no tapes in those days). These illustrated the events of that momentous day. He rushed to the BBC Normandy transmitter at Christmas Pie village between Guildford and Aldershot, and sat down at the microphone prepared to send his report up the line to London, although he was obviously utterly exhausted after such a long and exciting day.

He started to speak and cued in his first disc. Absolute silence. There was nothing on it. He tried with another and another. But it was the same with them all. Something must have gone wrong with his recording machine. They were all blank. You can imagine how he felt. Muttering a few 'well-chosen words' to himself he sat down at a desk and wrote for nearly two hours, putting on paper what should have been on the discs. When he had finished he then recorded a half-hour talk up the line to London. It was typical of his industry and dedication.

I mentioned just now 'a few well-chosen words'. In fact Richard, although he could wax indignant at some official pomposity or administrative blunder, never really lost his temper. But he did have one piece of bad luck which caused him to hit the headlines in the press. It was during the Queen's visit to Berlin and BBC Television was there to broadcast this historic occasion. But there were a lot of technical problems with the lines which meant that the broadcast started six minutes late. Richard started off and was going splendidly when a message came through from London that they were not receiving the broadcast. They said they were getting neither sound nor vision. Dick Francis, the producer, said to Richard through his headphones, 'Hold everything. We're not on the air. London isn't getting us.' Richard was naturally exasperated after giving of his best.

'Jesus wept,' he said, not thinking he was on the air. But for some reason, in spite of the messages to the contrary, London *had* been receiving the broadcast perfectly and Richard's words had gone into every home in Great Britain. The BBC had to issue an apology as every paper headlined the story. Most were highly critical but the *Daily Mirror* probably summed up best the feeling of the average viewer: 'So he *is* human after all,' was their comment.

In addition to our Monte Carlo trip together I was lucky to work with Richard on a number of important television broadcasts. He handed over direct to me at the King's funeral when he was in St James's Street and I was at Hyde Park Corner. When the Queen and Prince Philip returned from the Australian tour in 1954 he was at Westminster Bridge, and I was half-way down Whitehall. On other occasions such as the Coronation and Princess Margaret's wedding I was stationed along the routes listening in my headphones to Richard's usual impeccable performance from Westminster Abbey.

The broadcast of the return of the Queen and Prince

Philip did not go quite according to plan, although as a result some people said to me the next day, 'You were very good. Your commentary was one of the best you have ever done, and nearly matched that of Richard Dimbleby.' High praise indeed! But read on . . .

The Royal Party were due to sail up to Tower Bridge in the royal yacht and then travel in a launch to Westminster Bridge. Here they were to get into an open carriage for the drive back to Buckingham Palace. Television Outside Broadcasts were to cover the journey from Westminster Bridge with Richard at Westminster Pier, myself half-way down Whitehall and Berkeley Smith at Buckingham Palace. At our conference beforehand it was decided that Richard should deal with the arrival and reception at Westminster Pier. I was to cover the journey down from Whitehall giving details of the horses, the carriage and the Household Cavalry escorts. Berkeley Smith was to describe the arrival at Buckingham Palace.

On the day it was foggy and the river was shrouded in mist. When the broadcast started I heard in my headphones Richard identifying all the people assembled to welcome the Queen. There was the Queen Mother, Princess Margaret, various ministers, a Lord Lieutenant, a mayor, plus the Guard of Honour of the Queen's Company First Battalion Grenadier Guards. Richard as usual was doing his job superbly, but did keep mentioning that the royal launch was still not in sight, no doubt delayed by the fog. Soon even Richard began to run out of material and, obviously a bit desperate, he began to poach on my preserve. He described and gave details of the open carriage, and named all the horses which had been given to the Queen by the Queen of Holland. When there was still no sight of the launch he went on to talk about the escort of the Household Cavalry, naming the officers, describing the uniforms and adding bits of regimental history of the Blues and Lifeguards.

At last the royal launch came into sight and he was able to give his commentary on the various presentations to the Queen. When the Queen and Prince Philip stepped into the carriage I heard him cue over to me as arranged.

I remember saying something like, 'Yes, the carriage is

just turning out of Westminster Square into Whitehall. . . .' After that I said nothing as it made its way through the cheering crowds lining Whitehall. When I saw in my monitor that it had gone through Trafalgar Square and passed under Admiralty Arch into the Mall I said, 'And as the Queen and Prince Philip reach their home straight after their long journey, over to Berkeley Smith at Buckingham Palace.'

In other words, I really said nothing because there was nothing to say. The viewers had heard all about the carriage, the horses and escort. They could see the crowds waving and knew that it was the Queen and Prince Philip in the carriage. So unintentionally I gave a lesson in the art of television commentary, which is never to say anything unless it adds to the picture. No wonder people said that I was good, even matching Dimbleby.

However, there was one way I could never match him and that was in cars. He had a succession of Rolls-Royces – always the latest model and, what is more, he was the first person in Great Britain to have a telephone in his car. He even beat Lew Grade! He often took his car on his various jobs in Europe, and it always caused quite a stir as the BBC commentator drove up in a Rolls.

For the last five years of his life Richard had cancer and was often in great pain when he broadcast. He frequently went straight to the microphone for a commentary after enduring painful treatment at St Thomas's. His courage was magnificent and he never complained. In fact he seemed to drive himself harder and harder with a work schedule that would have shattered most fit men. When it was obvious in the summer of 1965 that he was not going to be cured, some of us tried to see whether he could be knighted before he died. No television or radio performer (as opposed to actors, film stars, authors, dancers, musicians) had ever been so honoured, although Directors-General, controllers and chief engineers had received knighthoods.

How right and proper it would have been if Richard could have been the first commentator knight. But it was not to be. Through Lobby we tried Buckingham Palace and Number Ten but to no avail and Richard died in December much loved and mourned by the people of Great Britain. They had lost their voice at the BBC. We, his colleagues, had lost a friend and the greatest broadcaster there has ever been.

Kenneth Wolstenholme

Most of the present-day commentators are far too young to have taken part in the war. Of those old enough some of us were in the Services, some were war reporters, and others did equally essential work as, say, teachers or police officers. But one commentator who was a bomber pilot and one of the original Pathfinders, actually won a double medal – D.F.C. and Bar – soccer commentator Kenneth Wolstenholme.

He had been a journalist before the war and afterwards became the pioneer of BBC Television soccer commentary. It is not as easy a job as it may appear to viewers, especially when the game is dull or play below standard. Good identification of players is essential every time the ball is touched by another player. So is expert interpretation of the reasons for the referees awarding free kicks. In Kenneth's time it was also necessary to have a photographic memory of all the incidents which took place, like a goal, an off-side or a penalty. Nowadays action replay makes that part of the job far easier.

In these days of statistics every commentator must be armed with an assortment of facts, either in his head or on notes which are easily to hand. These must include such things as the teams' places in the League and Cup, the careers of individual players, and the historical details of each club and the grounds. Kenneth was very good at this, partly because he concentrated on the one sport. His main strength was the reading of a game and the ability to anticipate what the action would be – or rather perhaps *ought* to be. He demanded a high standard of play and could be a severe critic, which perhaps did not endear him to everyone. But he was honest.

He left the BBC in 1972 because they would not guarantee him coverage of the top games. I can quite understand his feelings. Having been so long at the top he wanted to stay there – or else. Since then apart from some regional commentary for I T V his authoritative voice has been sadly lost to soccer.

John Ellison

I have said that when I first joined O.B.s in 1946 I was allotted to John Ellison as his assistant in the many live outside broadcasts which we did from theatres and music halls in those days. Having been an actor before joining the B B C, he taught me the difficult art of timing and fitting what one had to say within a given time. This was especially important in broadcasts from theatres where the commentator had to try to describe the scene and the entries and exits of actors and actresses without interrupting the dialogue on stage.

John was small, dapper and good-looking, in spite of a car accident which ended his R A F career, and left the right side of his face paralysed. From the start I shared an office with him, which, because we were fairly junior, had no carpet. (By such things was seniority symbolized in the B B C at that time.) This is why it was so ideal for our office cricket game which we used to play in the lunch hour or during the odd slack period. For this we had a miniature cricket bat, a squash ball and a waste-paper basket for the wicket. The room was just big enough to have three a side and we scored four if the ball hit the wall and six if it hit the ceiling full tilt. For the sake of the people below we refrained from running up and down the pitch so the only scoring was by boundaries. The batsman could be caught off either the ceiling or the wall or if the ball landed in the 'in' or 'out' tray. (We had an L B W tray too – Let the Blighters Wait.)

Since there was no room for a run-up, the bowling had to be under-arm and not too fast, but it was possible to get terrific spin on the ball and scoring was harder than you might imagine. Our secretary, Polly Polden, whose desk was at square leg, was called on to be both official scorer and umpire and once the word had got around we had many visiting players to our room, among them Denis Compton, Bill Edrich and the Bedser twins. Our regular opponents were Stewart Macpherson, Wynford Vaughan-Thomas and Geoffrey Peck, who earned the nickname 'Slasher' because of his occasional brilliant bouts of hitting, during which Polly would duck down behind her typewriter and Stewart, who wore glasses, would shelter behind my desk, in the gully.

John was the most consistent bat; Wynford who bowled from half-way down the wicket, the most successful bowler. I was rather inconsistent since I used to practise commentating while I was batting and found it rather difficult to do both at the same time. Once or twice the telephone rang and the callers were asked to hold on till the end of the over – a request which they no doubt found puzzling!

We used to keep an ear open for Lobby's footsteps and when from time to time he did walk in the bat and ball had been swiftly hidden and the players were gathered in front of the wicket pretending to be deep in discussion. I'm sure he guessed what we were up to since we would all be in shirt sleeves and sometimes rather hot and breathless, but he was always very patient and tolerant. The game sadly came to an end two years later when, on my return from my honeymoon, I found that John and I had each been moved into tiny offices and our old room, now carpeted, given to a senior member of the department.

After about three or four years John left the staff and went freelance, and concentrated more on interviews and the presentation of shows like *Top of The Form*. This meant that I was left in charge of all the showbiz side of O.B.s but partly due to expense and the coming of television, live radio broadcasts from theatres gradually died out. The expense became prohibitive partly because of the increased payments for the musicians in the orchestra but also for dancers in the chorus who, though unseen and unheard in a radio broadcast, still had to be paid so much per head – or foot.

John had a pleasant, friendly voice which once earned him the billing of 'the commentator with a smile in his voice'. This warm personality stood him in good stead when he became the presenter for many years of *In Town Tonight*. In the days before television covered the whole country,

I.T.T. was a prestige programme with many millions of listeners every Saturday night. Any famous personality or stage or film star visiting Britain would automatically appear on it. It was, in this sense, the Michael Parkinson Show of the radio. But there the similarity ended as every word of everyone interviewed was scripted and, what is more, rehearsed beforehand. Unbelievable, but true. In spite of it, John made it all sound very natural. But it had its dangers. One Saturday night Danny Kaye, then the darling of the Palladium, was appearing in the programme and playing the fool in the control room while awaiting his turn. The person to be interviewed before him was Lord Rootes, of Rootes cars. John was just about to start to interview him when Danny Kaye rushed into the studio, picked up Lord Rootes's script, and flung it in the air, scattering the pages all over the floor. John and Lord Rootes were sitting opposite each other at a table, so they could not share a script, and an assistant had to rush in with another. Lord Rootes was not too pleased – nor would I have been – but John remained calm and somehow started the interview without the listeners suspecting anything.

One rare occasion when I appeared in the studio during my four years on 'Let's Go Somewhere' was when a Saturday fell on 1 April. We decided to make an April Fool of John, and tried to find someone who could imitate my voice. It wasn't easy. We tested one or two impersonators including Peter Cavanagh, 'The voice of them all'. But none of them seemed to get me right, until we were told of an up-and-coming young mimic who might do it. He came up to the BBC and after spending an hour talking to me had soon got my stupid giggle to perfection. His name was Peter Sellers.

So on the night I hid behind a screen in the studio and Peter went out into Oxford Street. John cued over to him ending with the usual words '. . . where are you tonight, Brian?' Peter picked up the cue in what sounded remarkably like my voice and started to interview passers-by. After a minute or so, he began to slur his words so that it sounded as if I had been drinking. Producer Peter Duncan, who was in the know, signalled to John to cut me and start the next interview. So John said, 'I'm afraid we'll have to fade Brian out as he's obviously not feeling well. . . .' I then walked out from behind my screen and said, 'What do you mean, John, I'm not well? I've never felt better in my life. April Fool!'

As you have probably realized, John was largely responsible for making my early days in O.B.s so happy and for helping me learn the tricks and trade of commentary. That has always been the nice thing about the BBC. Everyone is always quite happy to help a new boy, although at the back of their minds, it must sometimes occur to them that the new boy might learn too much, and ultimately take *their* place.

Bryon Butler

Among BBC commentators there seems to be a close affinity with the *Daily Telegraph* – Howard Marshall, Jim Swanton, Rex Alston and Bryon Butler all worked for both. Except for Rex Alston they were all journalists before they became commentators.

Bryon Butler is a West Countryman. Born in Taunton in 1934, he was educated at Taunton School and did his national service with the Somerset Light Infantry. His newspaper apprenticeship took him from Taunton to Exeter, Nottingham and Leicester. His first job in Fleet Street was with the *News Chronicle* which promptly closed after he had been with it for sixty days. He claims he was in no way responsible for its demise! He then freelanced for a while, sub-editing for the *Times*, reporting on rugby for the *Guardian* and writing features for the *Daily Express*. In 1960 he did his first freelance job for the BBC's Sports Department under Angus Mackay. He spent six years with the *Daily Telegraph*, writing on cricket and soccer, before joining the BBC staff in 1968, when he took over from Brian Moore as the Association Football correspondent.

So before joining the BBC he had had no commentary experience and was thrown in at the deep end, learning as he went along, as so many of us have done. He is now, of course, one of radio's top commentators, with a crisp, staccato style. His varied journalistic experiences make his reports on matches, or soccer's news stories, punchy and full of telling phrases. More than any other commentator, perhaps, he seems to speak in 'headlines' over the air, without resorting to clichés.

In 1969 he was brought near to tears at the end of a match on which he had been commentating. Leeds United had only to draw with Liverpool at Anfield to win the League Championship; but if they had lost, Liverpool would have been the champions. The score was a draw and Bryon was apprehensive of the reaction of the naturally disappointed Kop. Would they boo, fight, or try to invade the pitch? He need not have worried. After a pause the Kop began to sway, the scarves were held high and the Kop chorus sang out: 'Leeds are the champions, Leeds are the champions.' A pleasant soccer story, for a change.

Bryon has come out with his fair share of non sequiturs, including:
'Wilkins pushes the ball to the left – a perfect pass – to no one in particular,' and 'Keegan was there like a surgeon's knife – Bang!'

His job is soccer and it has taken him all over the world to about sixty countries, but I have a feeling that Bryon's first love is cricket. He plays it whenever he can and says his greatest sacrifice was when he was reporting on cricket six days a week throughout the summer for the *Daily Telegraph.* The seventh day was the only free time he had to play cricket, but he gave it up for those six years to spend Sundays with his family. And despite his successful professional career, his finest hour is still the moment when, with the last ball of the last over, he scored the vital two runs needed for a victory over Taunton's arch-rivals, Blundell's, and was carried shoulder-high off the pitch by cheering Taunton supporters.

Godfrey Talbot

Godfrey Talbot must be unique among commentators in two ways. First, he once did a commentary on a grand procession to the banks of the Ganges from the top of an elephant. Secondly, he must be the only commentator to make a fortune; and this was *after* retiring from broadcasting. He began as a journalist on the *Yorkshire Post, Manchester City*

News and the *Daily Dispatch*. He then joined the BBC as a reporter in 1937 and was one of the best-known of the BBC war correspondents throughout the war. For the rest of his career until he retired in 1969 he was the BBC's court correspondent or, as they discreetly called it, 'official BBC observer accredited to Buckingham Palace'. From then on no royal occasion and no royal tour was complete without him – hence the elephant-based commentary.

I can think of no one better suited for the job. Tall, good-looking, distinguished, well dressed, dignified, with the extra, essential ingredient of a delightful sense of humour. You could never imagine him making a gaffe like us other lesser mortals, and so far as I know he never did. But he has memories of one or two overseas colleagues on royal tours who coined quaint phrases: 'Here comes the Queen, fully-clothed and looking very decent.'

Or, of the Duke of Edinburgh: 'Number one Fella belong to Elizabeth. He has put his best sailor suit on.'

Godfrey also had the ideal voice, quiet, friendly and authoritative, and although obviously respectful, never overdid the flattery and obsequiousness. He always gave the impression that he was 'in the know' about goings-on at the Palace, and enlightened his commentaries and reports with harmless little bits of behind-the-scenes gossip.

His twenty-one years 'at Court' stood him in good stead when he finally retired from the BBC staff, and accounts for the fortune he has earned from his books on the Royal Family. All of them have been best-sellers both in Great Britain and overseas. Whereas we humble authors are delighted with sales of ten, twenty or even thirty thousand, Godfrey's have regularly topped six figures – books such as *Queen Elizabeth the Queen Mother*, *Royal Heritage* and the *Country Life Book of the Royal Family*. As he so rightly points out, a lot of this so-called fortune has gone to the taxman. But luckily, enough of it is left for him to enjoy for many more years his favourite recreation as revealed in *Who's Who* – 'keeping quiet'.

Henry Longhurst

If I had to pick out my favourite commentator on any sport – an invidious task – I think I would pick Henry Longhurst.

Like John Arlott in cricket and Dan Maskell at lawn tennis, he indelibly imprinted his personality and individual style on golf. It is significant that all three specialized in one sport on which they were an authority, not only on the skill and laws of the game, but even more perhaps on its history, traditions and personalities.

Commentary on cricket and lawn tennis had been broadcast on television and radio before the war. In golf there were some brilliant reports and comments by that great writer, Bernard Darwin. There were also a few attempts at describing the play, including Henry himself on the British Amateur Championships in 1935. But after the war golf was a virtual newcomer – especially to television, whereas now, thanks to the pioneer work done by Henry, it has become one of the top television sports.

Henry had many achievements during his varied life. He captained the Cambridge University golf team to victory in 1931. During the war for a short time he became a Member of Parliament. He wrote one thousand consecutive pieces for the *Sunday Times* as their golf correspondent for forty-five years. In 1965 he became the first Briton to work regularly for the American networks. He was awarded the CBE and in 1969 was given the Journalist of the Year Special Award. But perhaps the honour he valued most of all was when he was made an Honorary Life Member of the Royal and Ancient in 1977. Although a very sick man at the time he insisted on going up to St Andrews for the presentation.

What was his secret? His style was ideally suited to television. More than any television commentator that I have ever known, he knew by instinct when to talk and when to keep quiet. Someone quite rightly once described 'his brilliant flashes of silence'.

His gruff, confidential voice, his slow delivery, his wit and the ability to produce the apt phrase on the spur of the moment, were just what the viewer wanted. He became the friend of us all and the kind critic and friend of all the competitive golfers. He knew their difficulties and could appreciate all their tensions – especially when putting. He himself gave up golf because he got the 'twitch'. 'Once you've had 'em, you've got 'em,' he once said. With a whispered comment he could make the viewer at home in his armchair feel that *he* was actually about to putt.

Humour was never far away when Henry was about, so I am sure he would not mind my telling the story of when he nearly sued the BBC for slander. Henry was a good liver and liked to 'fortify' himself from time to time – not just in the club-house bar. Remember that he often had to stay at the top of the scaffolding tower which held the BBC commentary box for long periods of the day, in the cold, wet or heat. On one occasion Jim Swanton was commentating on television during a Test Match at Headingley. We were sharing air time with the Golf Open Championship, and half-way through the morning our producer told Jim to hand over to Henry at Lytham St Annes. This Jim did, ending with the words: 'So over now to Henry Longhurst.' Jim then turned to our summarizer Denis Compton and said, '. . . and I bet he's got his bottle of gin up there with him at the top of the tower.'

Unfortunately Jim spoke before his microphone had been switched off, so that Henry and all the millions of viewers heard his remark. Henry was naturally not too pleased, and had it not been his old friend Jim Swanton with whom he used to share a flat before the war, he might well have taken some sort of action for defamation of character.

It was a tribute to Henry's style that he was as popular in the United States as in Great Britain. The golf commentator's job is not easy. He has to speak against a background of silence, so that his every word is like dropping a pebble on to a still pond. Rugby, racing and soccer commentators can all get away with the slight fluff or not-so-perfect English, against the noise of the crowd. But in golf, lawn tennis, snooker and of course cricket, a mistake seems to be magnified by the backdrop of silence.

Henry was as near perfect as any commentator could be, even towards the end when he was sadly struggling against ill health. He was humble but at the same time a great deflater of pomposity. He died aged sixty-nine and in his last year made a typical comment: 'Three under-fours – not a bad score in the circumstances.' When ill health finally forced him to retire from work, he wrote: 'Now it is time to lay down my pen and alas the microphone too, and to reflect in whatever time may be left how uncommonly lucky I have been.'

What a lovely thing to have been able to write at the end of a successful and happy life. As one of his obituaries remarked about his CBE – he was a Commentator Beyond Excellence.

Dan Maskell

'The Voice of Tennis' began broadcasting on radio in 1949 and then took over from Freddy Grisewood as the main television commentator in 1951. He is one of those who has specialized in just one sport which in fact has been his life's work. He started as a ballboy at Queen's Club in 1923 and later became the professional at the club. He was coach to the All England Club at Wimbledon for twenty-seven years, coached the British Davis Cup team for sixteen years, including during its victorious years in the 1930s, when it won the Cup four years running from 1933 to 1936. He was British Professional Champion when aged only nineteen. Because he has been a professional all his life he was never able to play in the Davis Cup nor in the Wimbledon Championships, where professionals were not allowed to compete till 1968. But he has not missed a *single day's* Wimbledon, either as spectator or commentator, since 1927.

He is a warm, friendly, avuncular figure, and one of the most relaxed of all commentators. He seldom gets really worked up, though with his high principles he must have been sorely tempted to 'blow his top' over some of the appalling behaviour on the courts at Wimbledon in recent years. He did, however, protest strongly when a teenager once chased Borg across the Centre Court: 'This is sacrilege,' he said, raising his voice ever so slightly. 'She's wearing high heels!'

He takes tremendous trouble with his broadcasts and does at least two hours' daily homework before setting off to the day's broadcasting. Each evening too he will watch the repeats and playbacks of play to make sure he is not using the same comment too often. After all it isn't too easy with tennis. What *do* you say? Well played, fine shot, beautiful stroke, and so on. I think he has found that on occasions he has too often used expressions like 'Oh I say', 'Oh, my goodness.' But like Henry Longhurst he is a good timer of *when* to speak, and with his deep knowledge and experience of the game, his comments, when made, are always apt and to the point.

When he finally gives up, lawn tennis – like cricket without John Arlott and the Boat Race without John Snagge – will never be the same again. Dan has provided viewers with an impartial commentary of what is happening and why. When he does criticize he is kind and constructive, and his good relationship with all the players enables him to drop in bits of useful information about what's going on behind the scenes.

He is an emotional man who expects a high standard not only from the players, but from himself too. Only once has he let himself down when he was so moved and overjoyed for British Tennis when Virginia Wade won Wimbledon in Jubilee Year. But no one noticed. He was just unable to speak a single word. For thirty-three years now he has been appearing on television, though to my mind not enough in vision. His kind, crinkly, craggy face reveals the true man. Long may he continue to bring us the atmosphere of strawberries and cream, cucumber sandwiches, fair play and good tennis.

After that I must just tell one little tale 'against' him. He, Peter Alliss, John Snagge and myself once appeared on Bruce Forsyth's *Generation Game*. The competitors had to listen to each of us doing a short, out-of-vision commentary on our particular sport and write down who we were. They hardly got any of us right, though one chap did put down the cricket commentator as Brian Robertson. But the final insult to Dan was when one of the competitors guessed that he was Virginia Wade!

Harry Carpenter

Harry has a style peculiar to himself with his short, staccato, clipped sentences. As a commentator he sticks to boxing and greyhound racing, but is of course more frequently on the box as a presenter with an attractive smile, whether it be Wimbledon, the Open Golf or *Sportsnight*.

At Wimbledon he stays in an underground studio (the bunker) from 11.45 a.m. to 7.30 p.m. or later. He operates in front of a bank of monitors covering action on all the courts and with his producer 'conducts' the proceedings, switching from court to court, giving results and doing interviews. Not surprisingly he has been nicknamed 'The Mole' and over the years has earned the extra 'comfort' of his own studio loo. He does virtually the same thing at the Open Golf but in far pleasanter conditions – above ground.

He was a naval petty officer in the war and then became boxing correspondent of the *Daily Mail*, also specializing in greyhound racing and speedway. He started life as a journalist on the *Greyhound Express* when aged only sixteen. But his real forte is boxing commentary and although he never boxed himself, his judgement and comments are highly respected in the boxing world. He uses his staccato style but never shouts or gets over-excited and is appreciated by producers because he is unflappable and never panics. Not even on the occasion when Frank Bough handed over to 'Your carpenter, Harry Commentator.'

Some points of interest about him – he prefers one-to-one sport to team games, always wears a dark suit and tie in case of blood being spattered, and is probably one of the few commentators to have received police protection – in 1965 after threats and accusations of bias against an Irish boxer. He is one of television's really professional operators and even earned the praise (since that is what it was) of Mohammad Ali himself, who said in a foreword to one of Harry's books: 'He's not as dumb as he looks!'

Eddie Waring

There is little doubt that if you mention Rugby League to most people they will immediately think of Eddie Waring. If they live south of the Wash most will remember him with affection and be grateful for the many hours of amusement which he has provided. For thirty years he was a legend even before Mike Yarwood made him larger than life. The ladies, especially, enjoyed his 'ahaas' and 'eees' and expressions like 'up and under' for the high kick ahead, or 'he's taking an early baath' for a player sent off. 'Ruggerby Leeague' was his life. He played it and managed both Leeds and Dewsbury. In his first seven years with the latter they went from bottom of the table to win almost every honour in the game, including two League Championships. So here was a commentator who definitely knew his game from hard experience.

He worked on a local Dewsbury newspaper and then visited Australia with the first Rugby League Team to tour after the war. He did his first television commentary in 1951 and retired in 1981, and was given the full leaving treatment by the entire media.

This cocky little man with his inevitable Trilby hat at a jaunty angle, and those twinkling, mischievous eyes, was a slightly mysterious figure. No one – not even his producers – knew where he lived. All his mail and contracts were sent to the Queen's Hotel in Leeds, where he had an office and held court in the bar. He kept his private life entirely separate.

I said that viewers south of the Wash would remember Eddie with amusement. He certainly broadened the appeal of Rugby League away from its traditional home in the north. But though they could never dislike Eddie as a man, most northern Rugby League supporters thought that he did more harm than good to the game. They felt that his light approach and treatment of the game overshadowed its undoubted skills, thrills and tough play. These all became lost in the flow of chatter and often hilariously apt descriptions of what was going on out on the field: 'They've got to keep their hands warm somehow,' he said of two hefty forwards punching each other. Or of a man temporarily knocked out: 'He'll be all right. I saw his eyelids flutter.' Even better perhaps was this comment about a man lying prostrate after a crushing tackle: 'I don't know if that is the ball or his head. We'll know if it stands up.'

Whatever the feelings of his northern critics Eddie will, I am sure, always be remembered by most people for the laughter he gave them and for his chirpy, cheeky approach to television. He will be a hard man to follow.

Maurice Edelston

Maurice came into broadcasting late in life. He joined Outside Broadcasts in 1969 when aged fifty and shared an office with me in Broadcasting House. He had been a schoolmaster and a writer and also had shares in a sports goods business. He brought great sporting ability to the commentary teams. Best known as an amateur footballer, he was also a good tennis player, and had kept wicket for London University.

As an amateur footballer he played for Fulham, Brentford and Reading and appeared five times for England as an inside-forward in wartime internationals. He was stockily built and a fast mover with strong, slightly bowed legs. He was a superb passer and distributor of the ball and made many more goals than he scored himself. He had the reputation of being scrupulously clean and fair, and had only one foul given against him in his whole career – a player fell over his foot! He went on playing charity matches until his sudden death in 1976.

As you would expect, he could read a game better than any other commentator and was able to anticipate many moves. He had a quiet voice and never appeared to hurry, yet in both football and tennis he always seemed to keep pace with the game. At lawn tennis he was especially easy to follow, even in a fast double with four complicated names. Maurice was much liked wherever he went, and his chuckle was infectious. He was a delightful companion during the three years in which we shared an office – on the few occasions when we were both there!

Robert Hudson

Of all the leading commentators since the war the most unsung and least known to the public must surely be Robert Hudson. This is largely due to his quiet, unobtrusive and retiring personality. He is, in fact, one of the very few commentators who is not an extrovert. At the same time he is probably the most conscientious, and puts most of us to shame with his meticulous preparation and research before any programme in which he is taking part. He is essentially the broadcasters' commentator. We know all the difficulties he has to overcome and so appreciate his great skill. To the listeners, however, he makes it all sound too easy.

After leaving the army as a Major in the Royal Artillery he did his first cricket broadcast in 1947 for television, and for radio in 1948. His career has mostly been with radio and he has mainly commentated on cricket, rugby and ceremonials. He has had two spells as an administrator, first up in North Region, as it was then, and later when he succeeded Charles Max-Muller as Head of O.B.s in London.

His commentaries on cricket and rugby were hard to fault for accuracy of description, and he made sure that his knowledge of the laws and details of the players' careers was complete: in cricket, for instance, whereas most of us rely on the brains of Bill Frindall in the box, Robert always had his own little black book full of the records of all the players in the match. Most of us stroll casually into the box half an hour or so before the start of a game. But Robert liked to take his place about an hour before, and sit there concentrating on the job ahead.

I always had the feeling that it was quite a strain for him until the first ball was bowled. After that he was a different person and sounded confident and efficient, giving a completely accurate account of what was happening. Although in private life he has a good sense of humour, it did not often come through in his broadcasts, so he lacked some of the colour of someone like John Arlott.

Before I joined *Test Match Special*, in 1970, Robert had become Head of O.B.s and given up regular commentary. It was in fact entirely due to him that I was invited to join the *Test Match Special* team when I was dropped by television. Since he had left the commentary box I did not work a lot with him, which is perhaps just as well. I doubt whether he would have wholly approved of all the fun and games which we enjoy in the box today.

I have said that he appeared nervous, and in addition to sponging his face before a broadcast, he was also a tremendous fiddler while commentating. He used his hands the whole time to pick up pencils, rubbers or bits of paper. In those days Bill Frindall used to secure his score-sheets to wooden boards with large rubber bands. These were special favourites of Robert, who used to pull them out and stretch them to their utmost limit. During one Test he had just finished describing a particularly exciting over, during which he had been fiddling away with one of the rubber bands. As Freddie Brown started his between-over comments Robert fiddled once too often, and one of the bands came off the board. As if catapulted it shot across the box and hit Freddie a stinging blow in the left ear. Freddie let out a yelp but, after a nervous glance over his shoulder, continued talking, not sure whether he had been stung by a wasp or struck by a poisoned dart.

In spite of his great concentration Robert did make one amusing gaffe, during the England *v* New Zealand Test at Lord's in 1969. The two teams were as usual being presented to the Queen in front of the pavilion during the tea interval. 'It's obviously a great occasion for all the players,' Robert said. 'It's a moment they will always forget.'

One rather unusual feature about Robert was that at the end of a day he tended to fade away, and due to his shyness seldom mixed or talked with the players. In one way this is not a bad thing, as it is easier to criticize someone you don't know personally. But it also meant that the players hardly knew Robert and often used to ask, 'Who was that giving that excellent commentary?'

I have dealt with Robert as a cricket commentator but he was equally admired and respected by rugby enthusiasts. He is, however, best known as radio's number one ceremonial commentator. He has covered all the big royal occasions and until he decided to give up in 1981, had broadcast twenty-five Trooping the Colour parades. The drill is always the same each year, but somehow, by diligently talking to as many as possible of those taking part, Robert managed to make his commentary sound different. As for the royal occasions his research and meticulous timing put him into the Dimbleby class. He is always cool, calm and confident, and although he has decided to give up the Trooping, I hope, for the sake of listeners, that he will be available for ceremonial occasions for many years to come. Whoever eventually succeeds him cannot be any better.

Peter O'Sullevan

Peter was born in the last year of the Great War, was educated at Charterhouse and then, because of ill health, at the Alpine College in Switzerland. He first came into prominence as the Press Association's racing correspondent, during which period he occasionally acted as race-reader to Raymond Glendenning. On 1 March 1950 he joined the *Daily Express* and, remarkably, has been with them ever since. He formed a perfect double act with Clive Graham (The Scout) and they continued this partnership on television when Peter became the first *regular* television or radio racing commentator to commentate without a race-reader. In contrast to Peter's stimulating commentaries, Clive gave his witty and expert comments from his ringside seat in the paddock.

There have been many fast talkers whom I have already mentioned – Stewart Macpherson and Raymond Glendenning to name but two. But in an exciting finish Peter must surely outpace them all. He undergoes a remarkable change in the tempo and character of his voice. When not commentating Peter is quietly spoken and hardly raises his voice above a confidential whisper. But over the last furlong of a race all this disappears. While the horses are out in the country Peter talks fast but in a contemplative sort of way with his voice staying at a constant level and only the occasional increase in tempo and excitement if there is a faller or a badly taken jump. But as soon as the jockeys reach for their whips and the race to the finish is on, Peter becomes a different person. An incredible succession of horses' names spill from his mouth in an ever increasing crescendo. My own feeling is that the television sound engineers have the effects too high against his voice, and were it not for the picture it would not always be possible to follow his every word. This in fact often happens on television and you will notice that in most sporting broadcasts which they cover the background level of sound is too high.

Peter has proved the point that to be a racing commentator you must 'live' on the racecourses. There is not time for other sports as in the days of Raymond Glendenning. Peter's racing knowledge is unsurpassed but even so he has to do hours of homework to learn the colours of new owners, or to associate a well-known colour with a new horse. It bears emphasizing that a racing commentator may have twenty or so horses bearing down on him at full charge. If he is at a course like Newmarket they are coming headlong at him. He not only has to decide which horses are in the lead but having made his decision conjure up in his mind the name of the horse with that colour, the name of the jockey, trainer and owner. Unless he spent his whole life with the trainers, horses and jockeys his job would be impossible. Even so I still think it is near to a miracle.

Of course in addition to naming the right horses in their correct finishing order Peter has to have a cast-iron background knowledge about the breeding of the horses, and their past successes and failures. The same with the jockeys – he can add to the enjoyment of viewers by talking about their personalities and characters, and their particular style and skill.

Nowadays Peter wears a large pair of horn-rimmed spectacles but this has not hampered his use of the large swivelling binoculars which race commentators use. I am sure that like us all he makes mistakes, but I personally have never seen him call the wrong horse home.

He has trained himself to hide his own personal feelings. You can never tell if he has backed a particular horse (which he does from time to time, following no doubt his daily tips in the *Daily Express*). Nor when he had to commentate on his own horse, Attino, did he show a trace of emotion when it won, though I believe he did reveal that Attino had a passion for Polo Mints and loved listening to the radio. Talking of backing horses he once gave a very good tip to punters. Saturday is a bad day to bet, as many horses only run because owners want to see them, and many of them are often not fully fit (the horses, not the owners!).

Peter can top most commentators in two things. He is always immaculately turned out and would, I think, get most people's vote as best-dressed commentator. I can think of only two possible rivals – Richie Benaud and Peter Jones – both natty dressers. Secondly, except for Raymond Baxter, he is surely the fastest driver – at any rate on the road to Newmarket for which he holds some unlikely record. Sportsmen tend to drive fast, especially jockeys and cricketers who have to travel several times a week over vast distances. In cricket I would back Brian Close and Ian Botham to get to most places quicker than anyone else, although the former would be bound to have one or two 'close shaves' on the way.

Perhaps the best summing-up of Peter O'Sullevan was given by the person who said, 'Had he been at the charge of the Light Brigade, Peter would have given rank, name and number of each rider – plus of course, the name of the horse.'

Bill McLaren

Bill McLaren is a bit of a paradox. I would say that he is the most universally accepted and most popular of all the television commentators. And yet he probably talks more than any, and so breaks the golden rule of 'only talk when you can add to the picture'. But I honestly don't think I have ever heard anyone say they did not like Bill as a television commentator and there can be precious few – if any – of whom that can be said.

He has a melodious baritone voice with a rich Scottish accent but is perfectly easy to understand. His rugby background is impeccable. Born and bred in Hawick, he played rugby for the High School and later for Hawick itself. As a flank forward he played for a Scotland XV *v* the Army, but his rugby career was cut short by tuberculosis. He was completely cured of this by the 'new' drug streptomycin and got a job as a rugby reporter on the local Hawick paper. His editor, John Hood, recommended Bill to the BBC without his knowing and they wrote a letter offering him an audition. He at first thought this was a joke and threw the letter into the waste-paper basket. But eventually he did a ten-minute test with five others. As a result of this he was given fifty minutes' commentary on a match between Glasgow and Edinburgh. His next break-through was when he was squeezed in for ten minutes between Rex Alston and G. V. Wynne-Jones for a Scotland *v* Wales match in the early fifties. He continued to do radio until 1962 when he began on television and has never looked back since.

He is respected by all nationalities because of his great knowledge of the game and his complete impartiality. He admits though that on one occasion his nationality nearly got the better of him. In 1969 in the Scotland *v* France match the score was 3–3 with only one minute to go. Jim Telfer then scored the winning try for Scotland and Bill's voice reached an unnaturally high pitch!

He owes his knowledge to a great deal of hard work, in addition to his playing experience. He does a tremendous amount of rugby research and, following a tip from Raymond Glendenning, prepares cards for each player and a big double-foolscap sheet containing essential details of the teams, grounds, referee, touch judges and coaches. On the morning before each International he reads the laws of Rugby Football. During a match he is therefore well-qualified to name the offence after every whistle, not very easy when a mass of players are lying one on top of another.

He has always been prepared to learn from other commentators. Richard Dimbleby told him: 'Collect as much information as you can. You'll only use about three per cent and you'll feel that much of your work was wasted. But don't you believe it!' So spake the master.

Bill also noticed that when Henry Longhurst commentated he seemed to be playing the game with the players. And so it is with Bill. He is the players' commentator who often knows what they are thinking: 'He'll be sorry about that,' or, 'He'll be cursing himself.' That's about as far as he will go with his criticism. But the viewer does often feel like getting out of his armchair and joining in with the scrum. Bill brings it all alive and is undoubtedly helped by his job – Supervisor of Sport and Physical Recreation in Hawick's five primary schools. Every day he is having to 'put it across' to young boys and girls. And not just rugby. Gym, soccer, netball and even dancing are included in his curriculum. No wonder he 'puts it across' so well to all his BBC pupils.

For all his popularity with viewers, his must be one of the least well-known faces among the top commentators. He is rarely seen in vision. He arrives at an International the day before the match in order to watch the practices. After the game whenever possible he catches the first plane or train back to his beloved Hawick. At least he escapes the mass of autograph hunters. They are not sure who they are looking for.

Max Robertson

So far as I know there has only been one commentator who has ever been a gold prospector – Max Robertson. He was born in India, and educated at Haileybury and Clare College, Cambridge but left early to join some amateur gold seekers in Papua, New Guinea. I am afraid that they were not very successful, so that Max ended up in Sydney, Australia, where his versatile broadcasting career began. In 1937 he joined the Australian Broadcasting Commission as an announcer and general commentator. Two years later he returned to England and became an announcer on the BBC European Service. During the war he was commissioned in the Royal Artillery (Territorial Army) and became an Adjutant, which gives a clue to his character. Max has always organized himself well, and has been punctual, meticulous, hardworking and self-disciplined. After the war he returned to the BBC, and although still with the European Service, broadcast from Wimbledon and the 1948 Olympic Games for O.B.s, whom he finally joined in 1950.

He will always be associated with his lightning radio commentaries on tennis, but in fact he has done a variety of television and radio jobs. For radio there has been the Coronation, a royal tour in Canada, a number of Olympic Games and some ceremonials. The latter included the occasion when the Queen of Norway arrived at the Guildhall for lunch with the Lord Mayor. Said Max: 'The Queen of Norway is looking very attractive in an off-the-hat face.'

Max's fast vocal style did not suit television commentary, but as he was possibly the best-looking of all the post-war commentators, he was much in demand as a presenter on television. He even took over *Panorama* for a short period, and his *Going for a Song* was one of television's most popular programmes. He was a natural for this as he is a collector of Chinese and Japanese ceramics.

Max and I have two things in common. We were both wicket-keepers (he kept regularly for the BBC at Motspur

Park), and we are at the time of writing the only two commentators who started in 1946 and are still commentating on the same sport. In fact I would say that there is only one other commentator who can beat us both into a cocked hat – the indestructible Wynford Vaughan-Thomas who began *before* the war.

Anyway, what is the secret of Max's success? Besides the usual hard work and research, and the ability to produce colourful descriptions of what he sees, he is quite simply the fastest and clearest talker on radio. I have already said how much I admire racing commentators. But difficult as their task is they only have to keep going for a few minutes. Max and his colleagues may have to keep going for several hours on end. Modern tennis too has become faster with the development of service and hard hitting. The real difficulty comes during a long rally in a doubles match. The commentator not only has to describe the shot but pronounce clearly the name of the player who made it. Just imagine having to commentate on a long rally in which these four ladies' names are involved: Navratilova and Mandlikova *v* Kiyomura and Sawamatsu.

But somehow Max manages to keep up with the play, with words pouring from his mouth at an unbelievable pace, revealing a remarkable co-ordination between eye and tongue. There has never been anyone else quite like him and I doubt if there ever will be.

Wilf Wooller

Another commentator who combined his profession with broadcasting was Wilf Wooller. BBC Wales have always covered Glamorgan's county championship matches extensively on television, and Wilf has been the main commentator for years. He was secretary of Glamorgan from 1938 to 1977 – the longest serving county secretary. He was a Test selector and journalist, writing for the *Sunday Telegraph* on both cricket and rugby. He captained Glamorgan in 1948 when they won the championship and was a useful all-rounder who played the game the hard way. He asked for no quarter, and expected none, and there were frequently little 'local difficulties' with opposing captains, especially those of Sussex and Nottinghamshire, when characters tended to clash.

His three and a half years as a P.O.W. in a Japanese camp made him an even tougher character than when he played eighteen times for Wales at rugby. He has been the most outspoken of all our cricket commentators, and a merciless critic of any bad play or tactics. At a home match on a Saturday he would often be commentating, writing for a Sunday newspaper and, as secretary, running the match. His commentary was often interrupted by a member coming over to the commentary position to complain about something like lack of buns or a dirty loo. He was a great advocate of positive play and on one occasion offered the crowd their money back after Brian Close had batted, he thought, too slowly.

It was sometimes difficult for Wilf to combine his criticism of the play or players with his main job as secretary. The Glamorgan team often learnt who was to be dropped in the next match by listening to Wilf's television commentary. It is said that in one broadcast he commented on a Glamorgan player: 'If he plays another shot like that he won't play in the next match.' But he was one of the game's great characters, and this came out in his commentary. He also could not hide – the microphone is a great revealer of the truth – that underneath all his tough talk and forthright views he was really a bit of a softy. And he made history with the help of a bit of luck, when Gary Sobers created a world record in 1968 at Swansea. Nottinghamshire were looking for quick runs before a declaration when Malcolm Nash, normally medium-pace, came on to bowl *slow* left arm at Gary Sobers. BBC Wales were not televising at the time, but something prompted the producer to start recording. Luckily Wilf was up in the box and so was able to describe Gary Sobers hitting six sixes in an over. It is one of cricket's most treasured pieces of film and it is good to hear Wilf's voice getting more and more excited as six followed six. He admits to losing his glasses in all the excitement.

It was a great pity that his commentating was largely restricted to Wales. Listeners or viewers in the rest of Great

Britain might have loved or hated him, but they would have realized that here was a commentator with character.

Nigel Starmer-Smith

Old rugby internationals seem to make excellent commentators, far more than old players from any other game. I can think of Peter Cranmer, Cliff Morgan, Ian Robertson, Chris Reay and Rex Alston (who although not an international, captained both Bedfordshire and the East Midlands).

And then of course there is Nigel Starmer-Smith who came to Radio O.B.s shortly before I left, and now does such admirable commentaries for BBC 2 Television. He gained seven caps for England as scrum-half or as Jimmy Hill once said, '. . . he had seven craps as scum-half for England.'

Nigel is very much the players' commentator. He seems to know what they are thinking and can of course appreciate from personal experience all the conditions and difficulties under which they are playing. He has a pleasant, cheerful voice and brings the game very much alive. At the age of thirty-four he came on as substitute for Dusty Hare for the Barbarians against the East Midlands. He showed that he had lost little of his skill and, for a commentator, was still remarkably fit, when he made two spectacular tackles.

He has spread his wings and now does some tennis commentary, and should be a regular on the television scene for many years.

David Coleman

David Coleman was the first and foremost of the modern style of commentators who surfaced in the mid-fifties with the swift development of television. He was always supremely confident, slick, smartly dressed and insisted on the highest standards. He was intolerant of inefficiency and this would sometimes lead to differences with producers and cameramen. But his intention was to be the best, and from 1954 when he first joined the BBC he soon became the top television sports presenter, linkman, interviewer and commentator. He also became the highest paid of them all and is still going strong after nearly thirty years. I think that he would agree that he has mellowed slightly over the years, though not at the expense of his confidence and desire for perfection.

Like so many sporting commentators he started on a newspaper, and was editor of a local Cheshire paper when only twenty-three. He was in the Signals in the war, and then joined the Army paper, *Union Jack*. He joined the BBC in Birmingham in 1954, and through *Grandstand*, *Sportsnight* and *Match of the Day* soon became BBC TV Sport's number one. Soccer and athletics have been his commentary sports and he had practical experience of both.

He was a first-class runner and was Cheshire champion for the mile and was also the first non-international to win the Manchester mile. This has been of great help in his athletic commentaries and he is a good reader of the tactics being used by the various runners. He is a fast talker and possibly, like most of us, gets a little bit too excited at times. But he is a good judge of pace and distance and always seems to call the right runners home.

David is renowned for his unintentional howlers. At athletics meetings he could say (of an unknown runner): 'This man could be a black horse'; or (of a rather short runner): 'He's even smaller in real life than he is on the track'; or (of a favourite who was not winning the race, as expected): 'He just can't believe what's not happening to him!'

It is very difficult when broadcasting from something like the Olympics not to appear biased in favour of your country. In fact rightly or wrongly I would say that most British viewers want to hear their particular champion encouraged and shouted home. Perhaps he did overdo it when David Hemery won a gold medal: '. . . David Hemery's first, Hennige West Germany second and who cares who's third!' (Actually Mrs Sherwood did because her husband John Sherwood of Great Britain was the third man.)

Perhaps his hardest and almost impossible task is the Olympic one hundred metres. He has had to cover as many as twelve heats at five-minute intervals with eight runners in each. Each race takes about ten seconds and there are names like Papageorgopoulos and Ravelomanantsoa. Try getting your tongue round that lot, and imagine the research needed to learn about the ninety-six competitors taking part in those heats.

In soccer he tends now to be more concerned with the discussions and interviews at the big match occasions. But as a commentator he is strong, fluent and forthright in his opinions. One of his little classics was once when talking about Manchester United: '. . . there are United now buzzing round the goal mouth like a lot of *red* blue-bottles.'

Ron Pickering

Another commentator whose profession made him a 'natural' as an athletics commentator is Ron Pickering. He was the Amateur Athletics Association coach for Wales and South West England and helped Lynn Davies win his Olympic Gold Medal for the Long Jump. Later Ron joined the Greater London Council as the recreational manager of the Lee Valley Scheme. He was born into a cockney family and his father was a boxer. Ron himself was a good athlete at school but abandoned his own hopes of winning a gold medal when his girlfriend beat him in the school long jump. It was not such a disgrace as it sounds because his victor was Jean Desforges who in 1952 captained England's Women's Team, and in 1954 was European Long Jump Champion.

Ron has always been a fighter for good causes – sports facilities for young people, anti-drugs, the Olympics in Moscow and starting the Harringay Athletics Club to encourage good race relations. The goodness of the man comes out in his sympathetic commentaries which, added to his vast knowledge of athletics and the athletic world, make him an ideal partner for David Coleman in BBC Television's excellent coverage of the sport. Ron has quite a large physique, a rather 'with it' hair style and a sense of fun. Viewers respect him and have confidence in him, because in the complicated variety of athletics he quite obviously knows what he is talking about. He is credited – or debited! – with one of the great athletics gaffes: '. . . here comes Juantorena now – every time the big Cuban opens his legs he shows his class!'

Peter Alliss

Peter Alliss has been a worthy successor to Henry Longhurst but in a very different way. He is the epitome of what people expect the modern commentator to be. He is cheerful, witty, gregarious and good-looking. He exudes confidence and not only looks prosperous but is! He writes about golf, he coaches and does interviews and is a course architect. Like Freddie Trueman he boasts a Rolls-Royce – P U T 3. But with it all he has a human and friendly touch. This came over well in his television series *Around with Alliss* which included a good 'mix' of partners such as Lord Scanlon, Michael Parkinson, Sir Douglas Bader and Bill McLaren.

As a player he won twenty-two major tournaments and played for Great Britain in the Ryder Cup. He was a stylish player and always looked better than his results. Even more than Henry he can sympathize with the tensions of the man on the green. For he too got the twitch, or 'yips' as I think he calls it, and once took four from the edge of the eighteenth at Wentworth which contributed to Great Britain's defeat in the 1953 Ryder Cup.

Since starting on television under Henry's wing in 1965, Peter has become the master at telling the average golf viewer exactly what is happening and why. He knows the players so well that he almost seems to read their minds. With experience he has learnt the art of being informative, descriptive and colourful in an utterly unpompous manner. He can build suspense without overdoing it, and realizes that the personalities and characters of players are the strings which a commentator plucks to bring the game alive. Peter is never at a loss and as someone once said, 'His putter is not too good, but his patter . . .!'

Tom Fleming

There are quite a few commentators who came into broadcasting after they had already established themselves in another profession. A good example is Tom Fleming, the successor to Richard Dimbleby on BBC Television for ceremonials and royal occasions. He actually first broadcast in a schools' programme in 1944, when he was aged only sixteen, in which by a strange chance he played a commentator at the wedding of the Dauphin and Mary Queen of Scots. But that was his last connection with broadcasting for at least eight years.

He had to do his national service and toured the 14th Army in India with an ENSA company led and directed by Edith Evans, being given the honorary rank of Captain. He gained useful experience by stage-managing the tour. When it finished he came back home to join the Royal Navy with no rank at all, but managed to stay on the entertainment side, even though he had to carry buckets of water to makeshift dressing-rooms.

This experience of life in the services obviously stood him in good stead, because he founded the Edinburgh Gateway Company and enjoyed twelve successful seasons with them. Later he became the first director of the Edinburgh Civic Theatre Trust and founded the Royal Lyceum Theatre Company.

So he was already a well-established theatrical figure in Scotland when he made his BBC debut in 1952 followed by the Coronation in 1953 when he was in Westminster Abbey. He had already understudied Richard Dimbleby for the funeral of King George VI and was stand-by commentator for the funeral and lying-in-state of Sir Winston Churchill.

In the last thirty years he has covered nearly two hundred historic events, including the Remembrance Day Ceremony at the Cenotaph on the last eighteen occasions. His father – a Baptist minister – was known as Golden Voice and Tom has inherited a deep voice with brown velvet tones. He sounds serious and dignified and speaks in the measured, revered way which the BBC seems to expect from the 'royal' commentators. There is little room for humour, though on Jubilee Day he spotted a young man wading in the lake of St James's Park with some object in his hand: 'If it's a sturgeon,' Tom said, 'he'll have to give it to the Queen. But it looks more like a rather wet shoe.'

He produces the required quota of purple phrases and his experience as an actor has undoubtedly helped him to learn and absorb a vast quantity of facts. As you would expect before a Royal Occasion, there are weeks and weeks of preparation and rehearsal. Every comment he makes must be apt, accurate and timed to perfection to coincide with the television picture. He really has a stupendous task. In the early days, when they covered Princess Elizabeth's wedding, the King's funeral and the Coronation, the BBC used to have commentators at various vantage points along the processional route. They would hand over to one other on instructions from a central control point. This continued until Princess Margaret's wedding in 1960. For the journey *to* Westminster Abbey I was one of the commentators on the route, and had a commentary position just by the garden of Number Ten on Horseguards' Parade. But for the return journey to Buckingham Palace it was decided that Richard Dimbleby should be the *only* commentator, following the procession all the way by looking at a monitor. So the cameras were still stationed along the route, but the voices of the commentators were silenced.

And so it has been ever since. One man covers the lot – the preliminaries, the processions and the service. For Prince Charles' wedding Tom was perched inside St Paul's high above the West Door, with a magnificent view of the nave, the choir stalls and the High Altar. But in fact he would be looking at his monitor so as to match his commentary with the picture which the producer would punch up on to his screen. This is where his timing has to be so exact. He may be describing the arrival of the Queen and Prince Philip inside St Paul's, when the producer's voice tells him in his headphones that Lady Diana is just leaving Clarence House. So Tom has to finish off his description neatly and steer the viewer back along the route to Clarence House with an appropriate phrase. Although he will have masses of notes, and will have marked up the march table of the processions and the order of service with essential information and titbits, he will have little or no time to look at them. Things move too quickly and he must store up all the essential details in his head. Remember that the BBC used *sixty-five* cameras at the Royal Wedding in 1981, which meant that the producer had the choice of sixty-five pictures to punch up on Tom's screen. And Tom had to be ready to comment on anything set before him, at a moment's notice.

These royal occasions are too important for the commentator to make a slip, however small. Everything, the names, the ranks, the recognition of V.I.P.s MUST be right. Luckily I have never had to commentate on a service, though I did do Trooping the Colour for several years for radio. A position along the route should be easy but I have never found it so, and I shall always remember my nightmare opening to my commentary on King George VI's funeral.

I was selected to be the television commentator at Hyde Park Corner, with Richard Dimbleby in St James's Street. We were naturally only given a few days' notice, but I was determined to get off to a good start. I felt that so long as I got my opening sentence right everything would then be much easier. So I discovered from Scotland Yard that the procession was going to be led by five metropolitan policemen on white horses. Each night before the funeral, just before I went to sleep, I said to myself: 'Here comes the procession now, led by five metropolitan policemen mounted on white horses.' Not only did I make sure that I knew it by heart, but I also stupidly wrote it down.

On the day, I was listening to Richard Dimbleby in my headphones as he described the procession winding its way up St James's Street. I then heard him say: 'The head of the procession should now be reaching Hyde Park Corner so over now to Brian Johnston.' My producer Keith Rogers said quietly into my headphones: 'Go ahead, Brian. Good luck.' So off I went, reading from my bit of paper. 'Yes, here comes the procession now, led by five metropolitan policemen mounted on. . . .' I then luckily looked up and to my horror saw that they were on black horses, not white. My mind went a blank. I knew it was no good saying white horses, because television at least had black and white in those days. So I limply continued, '. . . mounted on horse-back.' At this my producer said quietly into my headphones, 'What on earth do you think they are mounted on? Camels?!'

So my perfect start was ruined and I took quite a few minutes to recover. But I learnt my lesson. I have *never* written out my commentary since then. Notes, yes. But actual dialogue – definitely no. And one other thing to show what passes through a commentator's mind on such occasions. When the cortege passed me I had to stop myself using a phrase often used by commentators describing a procession. I had to keep saying to myself: 'Don't say it, don't say it.' Luckily I did not, since the phrase was: 'Here comes the main body of the procession.'

I'm afraid I have digressed, but the digression has not been wasted if it shows what a very difficult task Tom Fleming has. Remember he is doing it 'live' – no retakes. He himself admits that it is dangerous, and I am full of admiration for him. So far as I know he has never made a serious slip. So picture him next time, a tall, bearded figure in full morning-dress in spite of the fact that no one will see him. It helps to give him a sense of the occasion.

He lives up in Edinburgh but is on permanent stand-by for momentous happenings, which makes him feel, he says, like a public executioner waiting for the summons to do the deed.

Peter Bromley

If ever someone was suited to his job it is Peter Bromley. From Cheltenham and the Royal Military College at Sand-hurst, he served for three years (1948–51) in the famous cavalry regiment, the 14/20 Hussars. They were then of course mechanized but still maintained many of the old cavalry and horsey traditions. When he finished his service he rode for a time as an amateur until an accident forced him to give it up. He also acted as an assistant trainer before doing five years as a racecourse commentator. In 1959 he joined the BBC under contract as their first-ever accredited sports correspondent. Cricket (myself and Christopher

Martin-Jenkins), soccer (Brian Moore and Bryon Butler), lawn tennis (Gerald Williams) followed in the sixties and early seventies with *their* correspondents, but Peter was the first of all. He added to his qualifications by becoming an owner, and then a consultant on horse-breeding.

So, gifted with phenomenal eyesight, with a clear voice and a sense of pace, Peter has for twenty-four years been one of the BBC's outstanding commentators, mostly on radio, but with occasional television appearances. You will have noticed that I mentioned 'a sense of pace'. This is so important in racing, especially over the longer races. It is no good getting excited too early and Peter will calmly go through the horses giving their placings, and mentioning as many of the runners as possible. All punters are listening for *their* selection to be mentioned, however far back. But as the race develops Peter gradually increases his pace and begins to concentrate on the leaders, or those whom he thinks still have a chance. And then in the last two furlongs or so when the race is really on, he will speed up his tempo and allow himself to express the excitement which everyone feels when watching a close finish.

I have listened to him regularly throughout his career and I have never heard him get the winner wrong. Even if the judge asks for a photo-finish Peter is not afraid to say, '. . . and in my opinion so-and-so just made it.' Often too – as at Kempton – his commentary box is at an angle to the finish, and yet he seems to outjudge the judge. He also reels off the second and third, and most of the other runners too. As you know, I feel that the racing commentator has the hardest job of all, having to learn and recognize all the colours and then apply to them the name of the horse, jockey, trainer and owner. It can only be done by living on the racecourses and mixing with the racing fraternity, and, of course, by the usual essential for a commentator – hard work. Peter, like most of the other racing commentators, will paint all the colours for a race on a board and then learn them like a saying lesson at school. Of course the big owners and trainers are easy, but nowadays there are more and more syndicates in racing, each with their new set of colours.

Whatever our particular jobs may be in the BBC, people always seem to think it is all glamour, good living and being present at events which they would give their eyes to be at. But for someone like Peter it is not the bright lights and luxury hotels at the end of a day's racing. For a one-day meeting he motors home straight away after his last commentary. But for a three-day meeting he will stay quietly away from the social life and do his homework each night. It is the same with Peter O'Sullevan. He is usually the last to leave the press box, sometimes as late as 8 p.m., because he prepares for the next day's racing before leaving the racecourse. How they do it, I don't know, especially as I am colour-blind. They must have fantastic memories to register in their minds the details of horses – sometimes twenty runners in one race – for all the races which they are broadcasting.

One interesting thing about Peter. He always has an assistant – more often than not John Fenton – who before the race will give the latest betting odds as they change. But even more important when working with Peter is to write down the names of the winner, second, third and fourth as Peter calls them out. He has been concentrating so hard that he often forgets which horse he has said was second or third and John has to thrust his piece of paper into Peter's hand as soon as the horses have passed the post. How he reads John's writing I cannot imagine, but he does, and is grateful for this aide-mémoire after a close and exciting race. Like myself Peter enjoys life and his job, because apart from his delightful family and the odd shoot or game of squash, racing *is* his life.

Raymond Baxter

After John Ellison went freelance I shared an office with a friendly gruff-voiced Scotsman called Doug Fleming, who in spite of having a bit of a temper, seemed to enjoy the leg-pulls and jokes. When the department moved into the new part of Broadcasting House, Doug had gone to Australia, and my new partner was Raymond Baxter. He had come into the BBC via the RAF where he was a fighter pilot in

Spitfires serving in North Africa, Malta, Sicily, Italy and with the Tactical Air Force in Europe after D-Day. So he was a well-travelled man, and when he left the RAF started his broadcasting career with Forces Broadcasting first in Cairo, and ending as Deputy Station Director of B.F.N. Hamburg.

He and I were fairly different in character. I try to be five minutes early for everything, he was always late and has given many producers heart attacks waiting for him to turn up for a show. He was extremely knowledgeable in all things mechanical and scientific. I am quite hopeless at both. But we both have a sense of the ridiculous and whenever we did manage to meet in the office, we usually had a good laugh. As a commentator he was a natural for all things to do with cars, rallies, motor shows and Grand Prix racing. Similarly, for any air show or display he was completely in his element. He used to drive as a serious competitor and commentate at the same time in the Monte Carlo Rally, a difficult feat which he did extremely well. His motor racing commentaries for both radio and television were high class and I have never understood why the BBC have not used him more over the last ten years or so.

Raymond is very likeable and gregarious and this enabled him to know all the racing and rally drivers and have many of them as close friends. Once again I must stress how this affinity with those taking part in a sport is of great help to a commentator. It enables him to add the odd personal titbits which put that extra something into a commentary. Raymond has a very distinct style. He is very precise in his pronunciation and enunciates every syllable deliberately and clearly. It was this, coupled with his knowledge, that made him such a good presenter of *Tomorrow's World* on BBC TV. He had the ability to explain the most complicated piece of gadgetry or machinery in simple terms which even I could understand. To my mind he was a great loss to the programme when he decided to leave it because of a disagreement with a new producer. He had always been a 'non-knocker' and – rather like in *Down Your Way* – liked to look for the good things. The programme's attitude to Concorde, which it criticized, showed the way things were going. The new producer not only wanted Raymond to cease being the sole presenter and share the programme with two others, but in-depth investigation was going to be the policy. Raymond was in favour of facts, not opinions. So regretfully he did not sign a new contract for another series.

Although he was the king of TV technology, the modern whizz-kids tended to think him old-fashioned. 'Dinosaurs were left high and dry when the world evolved away from them,' said the new producer unkindly in explaining his reason for changing Raymond's role as chief presenter. If old-fashioned meant being courteous, fair and good mannered in his handling of people whom he interviewed on the programme then Raymond certainly *was* old-fashioned – and rightly proud of it.

I suppose that one of his most traumatic experiences was on Boxing Day 1956 when he and I were broadcasting for radio from Bertram Mills' Circus at Olympia. Raymond was doing the commentary on the various acts as they performed in the ring. I was just outside the entrance to the ring interviewing various artists before they went in to perform. Towards the end of the show I had just finished an interview with Bernard Mills and handed back to Raymond at the ringside for the next act which was a man on a motor-bike riding round and round inside a giant cage suspended about thirty feet above the ring. I remember saying to Bernard that he was my last interview, but just in case something went wrong with the timing of the broadcast and they decided to come over to me again, could he have some animal handy. We would at least have something to talk about.

Meanwhile in my headphones I heard Raymond describing the terrifying feats of the motor cyclist. Terrifying, because at the bottom of the cage was a large hole. So long as the rider kept going at a certain pace all was well. His bike went over the gap. But I heard Raymond say that if by chance his speed slackened then the bike would fall through the hole into the ring below. As he was saying this I saw the rider take one of his hands off his handlebars, and start taking off his jacket with his free hand. It looked dangerous and it was, steering the bike with one hand and circling round the cage at what looked a great speed. As he tried to remove his coat it trailed behind him, and must accidentally have got caught in his rear wheel. Anyhow, his engine suddenly stalled and to screams from the audience, he plunged through the gap into the ring. All this time Raymond was describing what was happening and of course was as surprised and as horrified as the audience when he saw the rider do exactly what he had said would happen if the bike's speed slackened.

An awful moment for any commentator, with the rider lying obviously knocked out in the middle of the ring, and Raymond knowing that he was going out live to an audience which must largely consist of children. He had to think quickly what to do. He decided to treat the incident as the 'natural' close of the act and said something like: '. . . and as the act ends spectacularly with the rider and bike plunging through the hole, let's go back to Brian Johnston for a final interview.' He had at least spared the children all the gruesome details of the rider being carried off on a stretcher by St John's Ambulancemen. Incidentally the poor chap died of multiple injuries about a week later.

As for me, I had been watching and hearing all that went on and was feeling pretty sick myself by what I had seen. However, I picked up Raymond's cue and looking over my shoulder, to my relief saw Bernard leading a white horse towards me. It was the only animal he had been able to get hold of in the rush, and was in fact a perfectly ordinary white horse.

'Yes,' I said, 'back here outside the ring Bernard Mills has just brought along a most interesting animal. . . .' For the next two minutes we waffled on about the poor horse, examined its teeth, four legs, fetlocks, withers, the lot. People listening must have thought we were mad, going on about such an ordinary animal. But I was keeping my eye on the ring, and as soon as I saw that they had cleared away the mess of the smashed bike, and taken the rider off on a stretcher, I thanked Bernard once again and returned to Raymond for the next act – a troupe of dogs. On with the show!

Eamonn Andrews

Most people, I suppose, think of Eamonn as a television presenter of such shows as *This Is Your Life, What's My*

Line? or *Crackerjack.* But he started life in broadcasting as
a boxing commentator. He was a middle-weight boxer and
a former All-Ireland Amateur Junior Boxing Champion. He
first broadcast for Radio Eireann as a boxing commentator
and then came over to England and for a dozen happy years
presented Angus Mackay's *Sports Report* on the Light Programme. They were a great combination, with Angus in the
studio whispering results and latest sports news into
Eamonn's right ear. So quick was Eamonn on the uptake
that the words seemed to go into his ear one moment and
out of his mouth the next. He soon got into boxing and
eventually took over from Stewart Macpherson as the
BBC's radio commentator, and in fact was not dissimilar in
style and voice to Stewart.

In 1951 he was asked by Peter Dimmock to commentate
for television at one of those posh boxing evenings, where
everyone wears a dinner jacket, including the commentator. He hired his evening clothes for the occasion and at
the end of the big fight was told by Peter to get into the
ring and interview the winner. He climbed through the
ropes and caught his hired clip-on bow tie on one of them
so that it came off. So for his first big television interview
in front of millions he appeared in a dinner jacket without
a tie.

It was a pity for the listener that he switched from commentary to television presentation, but of course it made
him into possibly the best-known face in the country and
certainly one of broadcasting's highest paid performers. But
he has not just stuck to performing and is by far the most
successful businessman of all TV stars, combining Chair-
manship of Radio Eireann's Statutory Authority with his
own private interests, including night clubs.

Eamonn is a deceptive man. At six foot, he is taller than
he looks on television, and still has a boxer's figure. His
main feature is his crooked smile and his main strength is
his affability, modesty and friendliness in dealing with other
people. He sometimes looks slightly embarrassed and believe it or not, after all his years of experience is still nervous
before a show. Although *This Is Your Life* is recorded nowadays, it was originally done 'live', and Eamonn still expects

something to go wrong. But somehow with him, it never does. A just reward for television's 'Nice Guy'.

Peter Dimmock

Television O.B.s owe as much to Peter Dimmock as Radio O.B.s did to Lobby. Peter was an RAF pilot and instructor during the war, and when he was demobilized in 1945 became the Press Association Racing Correspondent before joining BBC Television Outside Broadcasts as a producer and commentator in 1946. Most of his commentary was on racing but it was as an administrator that he really made his name. Up to the mid-fifties, however, he must have produced as many television O.B.s as anyone.

I know that in 1950 he was producing at our first-ever televised Test Match from Trent Bridge. At that time he was in his late twenties and was brash, supremely confident and never believed in taking 'no' from anybody. In this Test we were due to start televising at 11.30 a.m., which was the actual start of the day's play. This did not satisfy Peter. He thought – rightly – that there should be at least five minutes before play for the commentator to set the scene, give the result of the toss, and to talk about the weather, teams and the pitch. Although he had been at Dulwich College he did not appear to know too much about cricket. But at least he knew that the umpires went to the wickets five minutes before play started. So he decided to go and see them and came back in triumph. 'It's all right. I've seen Frank Chester and Harry Elliot and they've agreed to come out at 11.30 instead of 11.25.' I told you he was confident! Imagine a TV producer being able to alter the start of a Test Match. They can – and do – arrange the times of horse races to suit television. But cricket – no!

Anyhow, I expressed surprise without disillusioning him, and of course at 11.25 exactly, out of the pavilion came the two white-coated umpires. Peter was watching in the control van, and in my headphones I heard him shout: 'By God, there go the umpires – they shouldn't be out till 11.30. Stop them someone – quick.'

But of course Frank and Harry continued their slow walk

out on to the field and the match started at 11.30, just as we started our television broadcast. Peter was quite unabashed, and thought that he had been badly let down.

From 1954 to 1972 he was Head of Television O.B.s, later on adding the impressive title of General Manager. He was a man of tremendous drive and enthusiasm. Nothing was impossible. No one was inaccessible. He would fight to the last ditch for anything he wanted and he usually won. He could be ruthless, tough and overriding, which all sounds rather intimidating. But although a lot of people felt they had been 'done' by him, it was difficult not to laugh and forget after it was all over. This was because Peter himself had a quick wit and a good sense of humour and especially in the later years he was able to take a joke against himself, and laugh.

He was always immaculately dressed in a rather traditional way, and he even had a watch-chain across his waistcoat. He had a military moustache, and often a flower in his buttonhole. He was debonair, dynamic and had a wicked twinkle in his eye, with which he won his way with the ladies. He created a TV sports unit for the first time and was responsible for the weekly magazine programme *Sportsview*, which he presented for ten years. On occasions when he was away, I sat in for him, and this was not without its anxious moments.

It was the early days of the teleprompter where the script can be seen in the lens of the camera. In those days to keep the revolving script moving one had to press a button in the floor with one's foot, rather like a dentist, or when you want to flush a lavatory on a train. I was a bit inexperienced in its use, and found that if I pressed too hard the script went too fast and disappeared from sight – and there was no way of getting it back. This happened several times, and I had to 'ad lib' the bit that had disappeared. I also found that in reading the teleprompter I was in the hands of Paul Fox, the producer, who wrote what he wanted me to say. On one occasion there was an item about boxing, of which I know nothing. Paul Fox and the promoter Jack Solomons were not the best of friends, and Paul had written into the script something which Jack thought was libellous. Anyway, at the end of the programme the telephone on the desk rang and it was an unfuriated Jack threatening to sue *me* for libel. I managed to pacify him, but decided that I preferred my cricket.

Peter undoubtedly made the BBC supreme in television sport, and determined to get all the big events in every sport on to the BBC screens. He was prepared to sacrifice all-in wrestling – he considered it an entertainment, not a sport. But he had to work hard to get major sports like cricket and soccer to cooperate fully. Just as with radio in the thirties, they were terrified that television coverage would ruin their gates. The minor sports were no trouble – they needed the shop window. Peter did most of the negotiations himself and was a ruthless bargainer and, needless to say, being Peter, usually won in the end. There's a marvellous story told about him when he was negotiating a television contract for Test Matches with the MCC. He went to Lord's to meet them in the Committee Room. (The actual figures discussed vary as often as the story is told.)

'Gentlemen,' he started, 'I'll put my cards on the table so as not to waste your valuable time. All the BBC can afford is £100,000. I'm sorry but I can't go any higher and that is my one and final offer.'

The gentlemen of MCC conferred among themselves for a moment and their Chairman then said, 'Thank you for your courtesy, Mr Dimmock, and we appreciate your candid statement about your offer. Would you mind going into the Long Room whilst we discuss the matter among ourselves.'

So Peter went and strolled up and down in the Long Room, admiring all the pictures and cricket treasures in their cases. After about ten minutes the Secretary came and asked him to come back to the Committee Room.

'Well, Mr Dimmock,' said the Chairman, 'we have thought about your offer and quite understand that with the present BBC finances it is the best that you can make. Unfortunately we still feel that television is a danger to our gates and we feel we cannot let the Test Matches go so cheaply. Although I know it's only of academic interest to you since you cannot offer any more, the lowest price we could have accepted would have been £120,000.'

'Done,' said Peter, banging his hand down on the table. Collapse of the MCC Committee but the BBC got the contract!

Peter drove his staff as hard as himself and was a fair and constructive critic of producers and commentators. But he was always aiming for a high standard and must have been responsible for the development of many of today's star commentators on television.

Since leaving the BBC Peter has been Managing Director of the American Broadcasting Company Sports Worldwide Enterprises. What a title! But it fits Peter, who in addition to fighting for the BBC, always fought hard for himself, and managed to get a good bargain out of them. He had a strong commercial instinct and knew his own value. He therefore negotiated with the BBC for what he called a 'decent award'. At one time, because he also presented *Sportsview* in addition to being Head of O.B.s, he was rumoured to have a bigger salary than the Director-General. But in the end his needs outstripped what the BBC could offer, so he left. Just one personal comment. He and I have always been good friends, and although it did not stop him being critical if necessary, he was always kindness itself. In fact when I got the sack from television cricket commentary in 1970 (more of that later) the only bit of paper which I ever received from Television about the sacking, was a short note in his own handwriting, saying how much he personally would miss my commentaries. That was nice – and typical of him.

Dorian Williams

Some commentators seem especially suited by character, appearance and lifestyle to the sport on which they commentate. Even though he retired after Olympia in 1980, I suspect that most people still think of Dorian Williams whenever show jumping is mentioned. I think it is fair to say that BBC Television made show jumping the amazingly popular sport which it is today. And Dorian was not only the voice of the BBC for that sport from 1953 to 1980, but his was the hand which steered the producers to the stage of perfection which we see on our screens today.

In appearance he looked distinguished and was always well and soberly dressed in clothes cut in that special horsey style – jackets longer than most with slanting pockets, narrow trousers, well polished shoes. Except for the first year he was Master of Foxhounds of the Whaddon Chase for all the time he was broadcasting. His knowledge of the horses, riding and jumping was unsurpassed and founded on his own experience. In fact he has written twenty-six books (three of them novels) about horses and the art of training, treating and riding them. He aptly describes himself as 'Equestrian Commentator' and for all those twenty-eight years covered all the big events for BBC Television, including the Olympic Games, International Horse Show, Horse of the Year Show and Olympia.

In addition to his expertise and close relationships with all the show jumping world, his greatest asset as a commentator was his enthusiasm. His favourite was 'Jolly good' and his 'Oohs' and 'Ahs' and '*Come* on David', 'Go *on* Marion' not only raised the excitement and tension, but often made the armchair viewer feel he was actually in the saddle himself. Dorian was unashamedly partisan, and admitted it, which is rare in a commentator. He was also intensely patriotic so our successes or failures in international events raised him to peaks of enthusiasm or depths of depression. He seldom made a mistake though he did once announce Lady Rose Williams as George Hobbs – in spite of the difference in their figures! He was always impeccable in his description and treatment of the Royal Family, whether they were watching or competing. But he did once fall into the trap we have all fallen into in our time – thinking his microphone had been switched off when it hadn't. He once said, as a member of the Royal Family walked forward to present a cup at the end of a show: 'My God! What a hat!' – much to the delight of millions of viewers, who probably agreed with him.

There was another interesting side to Dorian. After he left Harrow he attended the Guildhall School of Music and Drama, was a schoolmaster from 1936 to 1945 and then in that year founded the Penley Centre of Adult Education at Tring, and has been a director ever since. And to show his versatility and that horses are not the only things in his life, every August he produces an open-air production of a Shakespeare play in the garden at Tring.

Once again I find myself saying it about a sport broadcast on BBC: horse jumping will never be quite the same again without Dorian.

Alan Weeks

The man for all seasons, and all sports. Whenever a minor or comparatively unknown sport is televised you can be pretty certain that Alan will be the commentator. He is always reliable and knowledgeable and has commentated on ice hockey, skating, soccer, volleyball, basketball, gymnastics, water-skiing, snooker and swimming. And I bet I have missed something out! I enjoy him best when he is doing dancing or figure-skating on ice. The technical terms for all the varied and intricate movements, such as double axels, camel spins and flying jump sit spins, just roll off his tongue.

It is not really surprising that he seems so much at home by an ice-rink. After leaving the Royal Navy in 1946 at the age of twenty-two, he became secretary of the Brighton Tigers ice hockey team, and general administrator of the Brighton Ice-Rink. In 1951 Peter Dimmock heard him on the public address system and gave him a test, which he passed with flying colours.

He wears rather large glasses and once after a football commentary he was called to the telephone. It was Buckingham Palace: 'We have just seen your spectacles on television; where can we buy a similar pair? They would be good for golf.' Now who of the Royal Family plays golf? I cannot remember seeing any royalty playing in public since Edward VIII and George VI, when they were the Prince of Wales and Duke of York.

Alan is so expert at all the sports which he covers that he is not often caught out. However, in the 1978 World Gymnastics he was commentating on Ronda Schwaudt carrying out some amazing movements on the beam: 'Whichever way you look at it,' he said, 'the improvement by the Americans is really quite – Aaagh!' While he was talking Ronda had mistimed a somersault and landed painfully astride the beam. He was also responsible for a little gem when swimmer David Wilkie was winning his gold medal in the Olympic Games: 'If Wilkie goes on like this he'll be home and dry!'

John Motson

One of the best of the modern commentators is John Motson, better known for his soccer commentaries, but who also now covers lawn tennis. He went to a rugby-playing secondary school, but learnt his soccer from his father – a Methodist minister – who used to take him to watch games all over London. He talks fast in a rather sad sounding voice and is full of facts and figures which he accumulated by poring over all the soccer records. He is accurate and objective and because he is a fair critic is popular with managers and players. He made his name on radio, joining their Sports Department in 1968 after reporting for the *Sheffield Telegraph* and commentating on local radio. Ten years later – as so often happens these days – he was grabbed by BBC Television for their *Match of the Day*. Radio is indeed the nursery for television.

John has been through the usual commentator's nightmares. In the 1978 World Cup the numbers of the Argentinian players were indecipherable against their striped shirts, and John had to commentate for twenty minutes or so without really knowing who was who. He has also made the usual gaffes. Once he was describing Tottenham's black forward Garth Crooks who was making space for his colleague Archibald: 'There's Crooks,' he said, 'doing all the SPADEwork for Archibald.' On radio in the 1977 Cup Final he said about Liverpool: 'If they lose today it will cast grave doubts on their ability to win the treble.' (The F.A. Cup, League Championship and European Cup.) Soccer commentary is not easy – unless the commentator knows his game and facts thoroughly, it can become just a recitation of names. There is also intense rivalry for the top position on BBC Television, and the feeling of a rival breathing down your neck makes the job that much more tense and difficult. But John seems to cope admirably.

Alun Williams

O.B. commentators could put on quite a good variety show. Wynford Vaughan-Thomas on piano; Tony Lewis on violin; Don Mosey – singing anything from Gilbert and Sullivan to *Ilkley Moor*; Christopher Martin-Jenkins with impersonations; myself – perhaps as a story-telling compère; Freddie Trueman as stand-up comic; and very definitely Alun Williams with songs at the piano. On many tours overseas he has entertained rugby teams, and on every sort of get-together where there is a piano, he is the life and soul of the party. He also travels round Wales in a professional capacity supporting such artistes as Max Boyce. He is fluent in Welsh and can tell stories and commentate equally well in either language. Perhaps because he was a permanent member of the staff in BBC Wales ever since the war, until he went freelance in 1982, he is possibly the most versatile of all modern commentators. There is really nothing that he has not had to cover, not just in Wales, but nationally for the BBC on big occasions. You can bet that you will find him somewhere on the route of the procession, whether it be coronation, wedding, jubilee or even funerals. He has the Welsh gift of language and rhetoric and also has the *joie de vivre* to bring lightness and laughter into his description of events. He also seems to attract around him every Welshman who happens to be in the crowd.

In sport in Wales he covers everything, including cricket and soccer. But he is of course best known all over the world – and in the Commonwealth especially – for his rugby and swimming commentaries. It would not be right to say that he does not sound pleased when Wales score a try. In truth, for a few seconds he is often hysterical. But one can easily forgive him for his enthusiasm, because of the skill and knowledge with which he describes the play leading up to *that* try. In swimming his famous '. . . he/she touches *NOW*' has rung round the Olympic pools all over the world.

He was in the Royal Navy before joining the BBC and as you will have gathered is a man of terrific energy, travelling many miles on his job ('Four or five times round the world'), and taking on far more than any one man should. He is a delightful companion to be with and a great story-teller and behind the glasses is the wickedest twinkle you will find in anyone's eyes.

He has had his awkward and embarrassing moments like all of us. I don't know of any real gaffes in English, but there have probably been some in Welsh which we don't know about. His fellow commentators remember with delight the Commonwealth Games in Jamaica in 1966. Lord Swansea won a gold medal for rifle-shooting and Alun with pride in his voice was describing the scene as Lord Swansea stood on the centre dais to receive his medal. Alun's voice broke into a near sob as the medal was hung round Lord Swansea's neck. But then to Alun's horror the local band started to play *Land of Hope and Glory*. Forgetting his BBC job, he rushed out of the commentary box and pointed out the mistake to the conductor. The band then tried to retrieve the position by playing *God Save the Queen*. And then – after further entreaties by Alun – they *did* strike up *Land of My Fathers*, giving Alun time to rush back to the commentary box to restart his commentary when the tune finished.

He has also had those dreaded long moments to fill when delays in a ceremony mean that the commentator has nothing to describe. This happened to Alun at the return from the round-the-world voyage of Francis Chichester, when he was due to land at a certain time at the steps by Plymouth Hoe. But Mrs Chichester – as she was then – went out in a boat to meet her husband before he landed, and there was a delay of an hour with nothing happening. Somehow Alun coped.

He was, however, struck dumb for some seconds on one occasion early in his BBC career. He had been commentating at the St Helen's Ground at Swansea on a county cricket match between Glamorgan and Lancashire. At the end of the game he had to rush back to the studio to give a close-of-play summary in a sports programme. Because he was then inexperienced he thought he would make sure to get off to a good start by writing down his opening sentence, and after that he felt he would feel more confident and he could then continue his summary unscripted. So he scrib-bled out something like: 'I've just got back from the St

Helen's Ground where in front of a large crowd there was an exciting day's cricket, Glamorgan bowling Lancashire out for 127, and then making 210 for 2 in reply.'

Alun had only time to rush straight back into the studio without talking to his producer first. Still, he knew that he had three minutes to do, and he had his opening sentence all written out, and the score-card of the day in front of him for the details of play. He had hardly sat down in front of the microphone when the presenter of the programme got a signal in his headphones, gave Alun a nod and said: 'Well here in the studio is Alun Williams, who has just got back from the St Helen's Ground, where in front of a large crowd there was an exciting day's cricket, Glamorgan bowling Lancashire out for 127, and then making 210 for 2 in reply. Alun.' As I said, he was struck dumb for a few seconds – who wouldn't be? – but he got out of it somehow and completed his three minutes. But like myself at the King's funeral he learnt the danger of writing down anything in advance when about to do a *live* broadcast.

By the way, he is a bit touchy about one thing. Alun – as you probably know – should be pronounced 'Alin'. Woe betide you if you cue over to him as 'Alun'. He will not start his piece of commentary until he has pointedly said: 'Yes, it's *Alin* Williams here.' Like myself, he is retired as a member of the BBC staff and now does just the same jobs as a freelance – and gets better paid too!

Julian Wilson

A commentator who tends to take a back seat is Julian Wilson the racing commentator, interviewer, reporter and tipster. But he plays a very important part in BBC Television's racing which he has coordinated since 1966. He comes from a fine stable as he is the old Harrovian son of Peter Wilson the great *Daily Mirror* sports columnist: 'The Man They Can't Gag.' But whereas Peter's specialist sports were boxing and lawn tennis, Julian has made racing his life. He is said to spend three hours daily on the form book and if rumour is correct, it has certainly paid off. Since 1956 he is said to have won over £100,000 after tax from betting. Certainly his tips in the morning on Radio 4 are very successful. He presents each day on television racing with Peter O'Sullevan and Jimmy Lindley and except when Peter is away, his commentary is largely restricted to analyzing the action replay of the last furlong or so at the end of each race. Not an easy task – to have to assess a race and pick out the vital incidents in a close finish at a moment's notice. But he does it extremely well, and his interviews of racing personalities are a model of informed questioning. He often has time for these interviews because the BBC usually only cover one meeting whereas I T V are generally at two. The BBC therefore have time to show the horses in the paddock before the races, an important aid to the punter. Julian is sometimes mistaken for Lester Piggott, although he is taller and – I'm sure he won't mind my saying this – his ears are bigger and stick out more. Still only just over forty years old, Julian is the complete racing man and will have plenty of opportunities in the future for more commentary.

Peter Jones

How versatile these Welshmen are! Wynford Vaughan-Thomas, Alun Williams and Peter Jones, put a microphone in their hands and they will talk and commentate about anything. It's not just the gift of the gab. They seem to have a natural exuberance and enthusiasm, and words stream out of their mouths like a waterfall. Long, beautiful words too. I honestly don't know where they find them. But if anyone can, then Peter can claim to be the *Roget's Thesaurus* of broadcasting. He has a pleasant, lilting voice to go with it too, which he often drops on the last word of a sentence.

He came into broadcasting late in life and like a few of us had that necessary little bit of luck which was to change his way of living. He got a blue for soccer at Cambridge in 1951 and 1952, and his captain was Peter May, who surprisingly captained Cambridge at soccer but not at cricket. Peter (Jones) also played as an amateur for Swansea under the captaincy of the legendary John Charles. After Cambridge he went to Bradfield where he was master in charge of soccer. Living nearby and playing for Reading at the time was Maurice Edelston, and Peter arranged for him to go and coach the boys at Bradfield. They became great friends and one day when Maurice was doing a soccer commentary for BBC Radio at Southampton, he took Peter along with him. After the match they had a drink in a pub with Tony Smith, the BBC producer from Bristol who was in charge of the broadcast. During the conversation Peter mentioned that he would love to have a shot at commentary one day. Tony promptly replied that he wanted a report from a match at Aldershot the following Saturday, and would Peter like to do it. Peter leapt at the chance and did a satisfactory job with his report. So much so that Angus Mackay, then in charge of Radio Sports News, heard it and offered Peter a job in the Sports Department. So Peter left Bradfield after thirteen years as a schoolmaster and became a broadcaster. Like myself, he happened to meet someone at the right time and took advantage of his luck. He was soon to make his mark, because Angus chose him to succeed Eamonn Andrews as the introducer of *Sports Report*, and Peter did this for five years, learning his trade as a soccer commentator at the same time.

He soon found that soccer commentary is not as easy as the commentators make it sound. The ball is constantly changing direction, up field, down field, and across from touch line to touch line. On its way it is passed from player to player. I remember that Raymond Glendenning told me that on average he could only mention one pass in three, unless his commentary was to become a list of players' names. And of course in those days there were the great players such as Matthews, James, Finney, Shackleton, Logie who tried to beat their man by controlled dribbling. Nowadays the players – because no doubt they are fitter – run all over the place and get rid of the ball to someone else as soon as they receive it. How seldom does one see a player trying to pass his opponent with a dribble or a dummy. This means that there are far *more* passes in modern football and it is quite impossible for the commentator to cover them all. Peter has therefore evolved what I call a 'thinking aloud' commentary. When play is in midfield and there is little likelihood of a goal, he will speak his thoughts as opposed to describing the game.

He may muse over what tactics the team is trying, what is going on in a certain player's mind, how the game will affect the teams' positions in the table, how the manager is feeling, and so on. He will do this for a few moments and then pick up the play again as one of the goals is threatened. Other commentators now do the same, and the soccer commentary is far less descriptive of actual play than it was. Were individual skills to be revived to the standards of say twenty or thirty years ago, then there would be something other than just passes to describe.

And that's quite enough about soccer commentary from me. But I did watch the Arsenal in the golden age of the thirties, so I *am* biased in thinking that soccer playing standards have deteriorated. Whilst talking about the Arsenal I must digress to tell you the only funny soccer story that I know – or possibly that exists, for that matter, because it is a fact that cricket and golf provide so many stories, leaving the other sports nowhere. Anyway, in the thirties Arsenal had a half-back called Copping who for those days was considered an aggressive hard-tackling player. They went to Italy to play a match against a well-known club and after about five minutes Copping whipped away the legs of an opponent with a sliding tackle. The small Italian referee ran up to him wagging a finger and said in broken English, 'No more of that please. We want a clean game.' Copping nodded but five minutes later did another vicious tackle. Again the referee ran up to him: 'I have already warned you once – next time I send you off – pronto.'

The game went on but Copping continued to play his natural game and soon had another Italian writhing in pain on the ground. Up came the little referee, notebook in hand, and as he approached, Copping muttered under his breath: 'Oh, bugger off.' 'Ah,' said the referee, 'that is good. You apologize, so I do not send you off.'

And now back to Peter in his many other roles, other than soccer commentator. He is now radio's number one for the big occasion, be it a jubilee procession, a wedding or a London Marathon. He is, I would say, happier outside than covering a service or ceremony indoors. He has one favourite expression which you can bet he will use at least once in any big radio broadcast. He loves to describe a person or people as 'walking tall'. This he physically does himself. He is tall, good-looking, with wavy hair and bags of charm. He is always debonair and smartly dressed and is in the international class as a chatter-up of the opposite sex! In addition to presenting sporting programmes such as *Sport on 2* and *Sports Report*, he has been chairman of innumerable quiz shows like *Sporting Chance*, *Treble Chance* or *Brain of Sport*. He also commentates on other sports including rowing and, of course, swimming where he has shone at many Olympic or Commonwealth Games, one of them producing the following classic phrase: 'Welcome to the Olympic pool where an enthusiastic crowd are cheering the exciting races which are taking place. I've never seen such excitement. It's the pool that sets them alight!'

Brian Moore

BBC's first Association Football Correspondent (1963), who went across to the other side, was Brian Moore. He went reluctantly at the time and tried hard to get a satisfactory contract with BBC Television, but failed. Not that he should worry now. He is ITV's number one commentator and presenter and is judged by many experts to be the best of the lot – either on BBC or ITV. His skill at both commentary and presentation is perhaps best illustrated by ITV's choosing him (their best commentator) to be their home-based presenter and conductor of their panel of experts through the 1982 World Cup.

Brian is different from most commentators who, as I have said, are on the whole extrovert and outwardly, at least, supremely confident. Brian is exactly the opposite. He is modest, diffident and retiring and claims to be afraid of meeting people. Not for him the sporting scene of receptions and dinners – if he can gracefully avoid it. He says he had an inferiority complex when he won a scholarship to Cranbrook School, because his father was a farm worker. But in spite of it, he didn't do too badly. He became captain of the school, cricket and hockey, and then got a commission in the RAF during his national service. So beneath that friendly, rather sad smile must be a lot of guts and steely determination to succeed in whatever he tries to do.

Why then, without the usual trappings of the successful commentator, has he become one of the top commentators in the country? Mainly because he has the vital factor of *knowing* his soccer and in a calm way commentates on the game with fairness and impartiality, and without too much of the frequently overdone excitement and shouting. When conducting a panel of experts he defers humbly to them and doesn't impose his own opinion too strongly, while remaining firmly in control.

So as I've said, Brian is an extremely rare bird among commentators. What's more he is a very nice person. But thank goodness like all of us he is human and does make mistakes. On one occasion he said: 'The referee is now looking at his whistle, and will blow his watch at any moment.'

Gerald Williams

If I were asked to nominate the commentator with the sexiest voice I think that I would choose Gerald Williams. He is a Welshman, but in his long absence from Wales he has lost most of his Welsh accent, though the lilt is still there. But his voice is sympathetic and has a beguiling and cajoling air which in his interviews draws out confidences – and sometimes indiscretions – from the stars of the tennis world.

He started life as a journalist when he left west Wales to come to London. He wrote for a number of newspapers not just on tennis but also on football. He finally became the lawn tennis correspondent of the *Daily Mail*. When he left the *Mail* he did commentaries for ITV on both soccer and tennis, until he joined BBC Radio in the early seventies and became their first-ever Lawn Tennis Correspondent. At first he did interviews and reports but has gradually become one of the BBC's top commentators. He developed his skills during his many assignments abroad where he has covered all the major overseas championships and tournaments. He has not got the speed of a Max Robertson but scores heavily with his great knowledge of the game and its administration, and even more important from his obviously close relationship with so many of the players.

As I write he is probably most admired for his interviewing, when, as I've said, he seems able to draw more out of his 'victims' than the other interviewers. In commentary he is learning the art of slipping in remarks between rallies which build up the tennis scene beyond just the game on the court. It can be a comment on the character of one of the players, picking out the wife or boyfriend watching, or just a throw-away remark about the weather or the strawberries and cream. It all helps to build up the Wimbledon atmosphere. My bet is – and I have no inside knowledge – that when Dan Maskell finally retires Gerald will be pinched by television from radio to take his place.

And yes, he *has* made a gaffe. I heard it myself during the 1982 Wimbledon. He was commentating on a ladies' doubles in which Pam Schriver was playing. She was suddenly stung by a wasp. It had obviously got inside her dress and Pam was peeping down her cleavage to try to find it. As she was looking down, Gerald – to fill in time – innocently remarked to Christine Trueman apropos of Pam and her partner: 'They are a fine pair, aren't they?' Incidentally, along with Jack Dempsey and John the Baptist, Gerald shares my birthday date of 24 June.

The Ladies: Audrey Russell, Judith Chalmers and others

Lobby has always felt guilty that he never developed nor used more lady commentators. But at least he was responsible for the first one ever – Thelma Carpenter. She was three times Amateur Women's Snooker Champion and gave a commentary on a snooker match in December 1936. Another first-class games player was cricketer and hockey international Marjorie Pollard. In 1937 she commentated on the England *v* Germany women's hockey match, and also England *v* Australia women's cricket. She was knowledgeable and extremely confident, and I had the pleasure of sharing a commentary with her once at the Oval.

Another lady chosen by Lobby was Olga Collett. She commented on the fashions at Ascot and on one royal occasion was heard to say, 'Someone in the procession is waving at me. Oh, no, it's the Queen acknowledging the cheers of the crowd.'

After the war Audrey Russell became a regular on royal and state occasions. She joined the BBC in 1942 as a reporter on *Radio Newsreel* and during the war reported in Belgium, Holland and Norway. Immediately after the war she was in the News Department, who shared her with O.B.s. But they soon resented having to lend her so often to O.B.s, and Audrey left the staff and became a freelance. She had been an actress and her clear, beautifully pitched voice was ideal for royal weddings, births and tours, the Coronation and the thirty Maundy Services which she broadcast. She went twice round the world with the Queen and lost count of the number of Royal Tours she covered. In 1952 she was waiting in Ceylon for the arrival of the Queen from Kenya, when the news of King George's death came through. She had to rush back for the funeral and at the briefing the night before remembers a friendly officer in charge of the correspondents saying in a voice sombre with grief, 'I am quite sure that everything will be tickety-boo on the day of the race.'

It was lucky that Audrey was not discouraged by Richard Dimbleby's advice to her when she was wondering whether to go freelance: 'You will never become a commentator – only men can do that!' But she added a much needed woman's touch to what, as Richard said, was a male preserve, and at last the female listeners got an accurate description of the dresses – including the occasion when she said: 'The Queen Mother is in dark black'! In spite of Audrey's experience and expertise she was often nervous before a big broadcast and had to be 'gently' nursed by her number two. There is normally a number two at every radio broadcast. He (or she) is usually a member of the BBC staff and his duties are to 'nurse' the commentator, more often than not a freelance. The object is to allow the commentator to concentrate on his job of describing what is happening, while the number two looks after everything else – the technical arrangements – liaison with those in control at Broadcasting House – time-keeping on the stopwatch – giving cues to the commentator when a new programme joins and, even more important, arranging for the odd cup of tea! Number twos are indispensable and contribute to the success of a broadcast.

I was very sorry – and I know how sad she was – that Audrey was not selected as a member of the BBC Radio team for the Royal Wedding in 1981. It would have completed a neat cycle as she had covered Princess Elizabeth's wedding, the birth of Prince Charles (not live commentary!) and the weddings of Princess Margaret and Princess Anne. But the home listeners' loss was a gain for those overseas, as she covered the wedding for the BBC World Service.

In 1952 Charles Max-Muller – then Head of Radio O.B.s – inaugurated a search for a lady commentator for the Coronation. Hundreds of ladies replied to his advertisement and these were whittled down to a final twenty. These were given a test which involved a description of the Changing of the Guard at Buckingham Palace. The panel of judges picked out Jean Metcalfe as an easy winner. She was of course already a well-known broadcaster in her *Family Favourites* programme every Sunday. She not only had a very attractive voice but was unflappable and gave the listener an excellent idea of what was happening. But somehow, due no doubt to the calls of motherhood and the demands of other programmes she never became a regular commentator for O.B.s.

Nowadays of course there *is* a star performer, someone you can trust with any kind of commentary, be it a procession, the Boat Race, a first night, a beauty contest or Ascot fashions. She is the warm, cuddly Judith Chalmers with the friendly smile. She is as nice as she looks and as sweet as she sounds. She really can turn her hand to anything, and as usual with good commentators never skimps her research or homework, in spite of having to bring up her two children. She is an exception among the ladies, in that her voice is easily recognizable. I don't know about you but in general I find it very difficult (on radio) to put a name to a lady's voice. It must be something to do with pitch, because on all the many phone-in programmes which there are today, every woman's voice sounds exactly the same to me.

On television it is different for obvious reasons, and at least in newscasting and current affairs the women seem to be gradually taking over from the men. But commentary both on television and radio still remains largely a male preserve.

Part Three Cricket

CHAPTER 6

I Learn the Art of Radio Commentary

Throughout the fifties and early sixties I continued to cover all the televised Tests for BBC TV. In 1950 Trent Bridge and Edgbaston came within our range when the Sutton Coldfield transmitter was opened. Two years later with Holme Moss in operation it was the turn of Old Trafford and Headingley, and our coverage of all six Test grounds was complete.

All this time I was learning the art of radio commentary, not at Test Matches, but at mid-week county matches, which the old Home Service used to broadcast regularly between 12 noon and 12.25 p.m. and from 3 p.m. to 3.30 with a close-of-play summary later. This was the best possible school. The commentator was on his own – except for a scorer – with no one to comment between the overs. This meant that twice daily he had to talk non-stop for nearly half an hour – not as easy as it may sometimes sound. Describing the actual play is fairly straightforward. But there are many inactive moments during a game of cricket, so this was a great opportunity to learn how to fill in during the time when nothing is happening. Not being a journalist, I also had to learn how to assess a day's play and put it all into a four-minute summary at the end of the day, something I have never found very easy to do, and which I don't particularly enjoy doing.

These county matches brought an additional bonus to an ordinary club cricketer like myself. They enabled me to meet and get to know all the players on the county scene. And I would like to say how grateful I am for the friendly way in which they have always accepted me. In addition, I was able to study the basics of first-class cricket – the skills, the tactics, the pitches, and even the subtle gamesmanship which is often employed.

The necessity to keep talking was of course in direct contrast to what I was trying to do on television, but I soon learnt to switch from one to the other. In one Test, however, because of the sickness of a colleague, I had to do both types of commentary on the same day, rushing from one commentary box to the other. That was *not* easy.

After I had been at the BBC for twelve years, I discovered that I was entitled to something called 'grace leave', which meant I could be given three months off with pay. So in 1958 it occurred to me that it was about time I saw some first-class cricket abroad. Rex Alston and John Arlott had gone on various MCC tours and joined the home commentary team in each country to broadcast back here. But this was very much on an *ad hoc* basis. There was no automatic coverage of any MCC tour by the BBC. Even when there was any coverage it was not necessarily from all the Tests and certainly not ball by ball except for the last two hours or so of play.

In 1958 Rex was in Australia for the Commonwealth Games and so was able to cover the first Test at Brisbane in early December. But there were no plans for him to stay out there for the rest of the tour, as he had to come home for the Rugby Internationals. So this was my chance. I applied for leave and bought myself a return air ticket to Australia. I was also prepared to pay all my own expenses out there. But when the BBC heard what I was doing, they decided to use me as a commentator and interviewer and to pay me for each job which I did for them. Luckily I was acceptable to the Australian Broadcasting Commission and they kindly invited me to be a member of their own commentary team for the four remaining Tests.

On 27 December I flew out of London on a BOAC Britannia and in those days the journey took about fifty hours. I had hoped to be given time to settle down and get used to the broadcasting conditions out there, but I was out of luck. People talk a lot about jet lag but I arrived in Melbourne on the afternoon of 30 December and was doing my first-ever commentary in Australia on the morning of the 31st. What is more, because Alan McGilvray's flight from Sydney was delayed, I was on second, twenty minutes after play had begun. Alan Davidson had taken the wickets of Peter Richardson, Willie Watson and Tom Graveney all in one over, and when I started England were 7 for 3, with Peter May, their captain, and Trevor Bailey trying desperately to hang on against the fast left arm of Davidson and the left arm chucks of Ian Meckiff. I had just begun to say how glad I was to be in Australia when a pigeon up in the rafters of the vast Melbourne Stand dropped a 'message of welcome' on to my wrist. Anyhow, it was a lucky omen, as England lost no more wickets while I was on. But what an introduction to broadcasting abroad!

I was soon to notice the difference between the techniques of the Australian commentators and the BBC. As I explained earlier, Lobby's instructions to commentators at cricket was to give the essentials first: the score, the weather, pitch, toss and so on. And of course to continue to give the score every time a run was scored, or if there was a maiden bowled, at least at the end of that over. After that we have always been encouraged to add 'colour' to our broadcasts. By this I mean descriptions of the ground, the crowd, and of course the players or the field. We think it adds to a broadcast to talk about the players' personalities and characteristics. There are also so many stories about cricket which can be subtly woven into the commentary, to say nothing of the many individual and team records.

In Australia it is exactly the opposite. They regard their main purpose as keeping the listener informed of the score and state of play. They are lucky to have had such a knowledgeable and expert commentator as Alan McGilvray over the past forty years. As a former captain of New South Wales he is a fine judge of the game and his commentaries are extremely accurate and to the point. But even he tends to stick a hundred per cent to the actual delivery and playing of the ball to the exclusion of all else. For example, over here we describe the man running up and add a few remarks about him – his style, his long hair, his recent performances or whatever. We then describe the stroke, where it has gone, and say something about the fielder. And then give the score. In Australia, in between giving the score comment is often restricted to '. . . and he bowls and it goes through to the keeper,' or, 'he bowls, and that's a single down to X at third man, and the score is now. . . .' In other words the Australian style is terse and accurate. Our style is more flowing and descriptive of *everything*, without, we hope, any loss of accuracy.

There was also the different way of giving the score, which at first took a bit of getting used to. When four wickets are down for twenty runs *they* say 4 for 20, *we* say 20 for 4. By way of compromise, what I used to do in Australia was to use their method when I was broadcasting with their commentary team to Australia only. But when the BBC joined us I would go back to our method. Alan does the same when he is in this country. The other minor differences are that they call extras 'sundries', and close of play 'stumps', but no one really worries which is used.

A newcomer to Australia, as I was then, also discovers that Down Under some words have different meanings from ours. I was once sharing a commentary box in Tasmania with a commentator called Peter Mears. During a pause in the play he asked me how I had spent my day off on Sunday.

'Oh,' I replied, 'I had a lovely day. I had my first bathe for two years.'

I noticed that he looked slightly surprised and edged further into his corner of the commentary box. It wasn't till several days later that I discovered that what I had said, to the Australian ear, was that I had had my first *bath* for two years!

CHAPTER 7

Voices of Cricket

Rex Alston

The majority of sports commentators have played or participated at some level or other in the sport on which they commentate. Some, like Harold Abrahams, Richie Benaud, Jim Laker, Nigel Starmer-Smith and Cliff Morgan, have been of international class. I must emphasize here, by the way, that I am talking about *commentators*, not summarizers.

One non-international but who qualified better than most was Rex Alston. He won an athletics blue at Cambridge and ran in the sprints as second string to Harold Abrahams. From 1924 to 1941 he was a master at Bedford School, and while there captained Bedford at rugby football and also played for Rosslyn Park and the East Midlands. In cricket he captained Bedfordshire in the Minor Counties Championship. Not surprisingly, his three main sports were cricket, rugby and athletics, to which he added lawn tennis.

Already you will have a clue to his character – a schoolmaster for seventeen years with obvious powers of leadership. He joined the BBC in 1942 and became a freelance when he reached retiring age in 1961. While on the staff he was the office organizer and commentary box leader in all four sports. He was precise, meticulous, fair, unbiased and demanding of a high standard of behaviour on the field, the track, the court and in the commentary box itself. He could at times sound like a schoolmaster, gently reproving any lapse in standards of play or behaviour. But he was a friendly, gregarious person and the commentary box was always a happy place when he was in command.

In my opinion, of the four sports, he was best at athletics, closely followed by rugby. At cricket he was – as we all were – slightly overshadowed by John Arlott. He was prone to slight mishaps and had more difficulties than most with the commentator's five-letter nightmare – 'balls'. At Canterbury once he described the scene during the tea interval: '. . . the band playing, the tents with their club flags, the famous lime tree, people picnicking round the ground, whilst on the field hundreds of small boys are playing with their balls.'

At Wimbledon during a ladies' singles match there was a slight delay and Rex said, 'Louise Brough can not serve at the moment as she has not got any balls.' I myself was guilty on one occasion of saying, 'Play has ended here at Southampton, but they play till seven o'clock up at Edgbaston, so over there now for some more balls from Rex Alston.'

When commentating Rex often held his head in his hands, looking straight out in front of him. During one Test when Jim Swanton was his summarizer Rex described a ball being snicked into the slips. 'I'm pretty certain that didn't carry so it wasn't a catch. But I'll just ask Jim what *he* thought. Jim?' As he got no reply he turned to his left and to his surprise saw an empty seat. On the desk in front of Jim's seat was a piece of paper which read: 'Gone to spend a penny. Back in a moment.' I cannot remember whether Rex actually read out the note, though these days, of course, there would be no such inhibitions.

Like all of us he made quite a few general gaffes. He once cued over to: 'Your next commentator, old John Arlott at Trafford.' One for which he cannot be blamed was in Australia, when he said: 'Lindwall has now finished his over, goes to the umpire, takes his sweater and strides off.' What Rex did not know was that in colloquial Australian, 'strides' are trousers.

Perhaps his most memorable statement was made at Lord's in 1962 during the MCC *v* Pakistan match. Pakistan's touring team included a player called Afaq Hussain, a name to strike terror into any commentator. On arrival at Lord's we all rushed to look at the score-card to check whether Afaq was playing. To the immense relief of us all, he had not been selected. However, I thought I would stir things up a bit, so left the television commentary box and went next door to find Rex in the radio box.

'Jolly lucky,' I said, 'that this chap Afaq isn't playing, isn't it?'

'Don't say that name, please,' replied Rex. 'I shall only get it into my head.'

'I quite understand,' I said. 'I'm as relieved as you are that he's not playing.' As I went out of the box I deliberately muttered: 'Afaq, Afaq, Afaq.'

Late in the afternoon MCC were about 200 for 6 with Barry Knight of Essex playing a useful innings. Burki, the Pakistan captain, threw the ball to a new bowler and Rex was heard to say: 'There's going to be a change of bowling. We are going to see Afaq to Knight at the nursery end.' When he realized what he had said and how his remark might be misconstrued, Rex held his head in his hands and said, 'What am I saying? He's not even playing!'

Rex is now over eighty but with his lean, wiry figure he is as fit as ever and still goes to cricket and rugby to write for the *Daily Telegraph*. His writing is as fair, his criticism as kind, and his knowledge and reading of the game as good, as when he was a commentator.

One final story about him. When he became a freelance he did his first commercial voice-over. It was for Andrex bathroom tissue and some bright person remarked, 'Well, if he's going to do voice-overs, he might as well start at the bottom.'

E. W. Swanton

Jim Swanton is a big man in both senses of the word. He has a strong personality, holds high principles and likes to get his own way – which he usually does. Some people who don't know him think he is pompous. So, I suppose, do his many friends, which is why we enjoy pulling his leg. On tours Jim had a habit of staying with governor-generals or dining with prime ministers and High Commissioners. I expect that he himself would admit that he was a wee bit of a snob. Anyhow, the thought prompted a now famous remark about him: 'Jim is such a snob that he won't travel in the same car as his chauffeur'!

Cricket has been his life and in addition to broadcasting he has written or edited about twenty books and been cricket correspondent of the *Evening Standard* in the thirties, and of the *Daily Telegraph* from 1946 to 1975. So far as I am concerned he wrote and said all the right things about cricket, and he made sure that he was given plenty of space to air his views. He also ensured that none of his copy could be sub-edited without reference to him. How his press colleagues envied him this unique journalistic licence. He was forthright in all he wrote and his often unfavourable comparison of modern cricket with that of the past did not always endear him to modern cricketers.

He began his radio broadcasting with some reports in 1934, followed by commentary on the 1938 and 1939 Tests in England. But his big chance came in the winter of 1938/39. He became the first commentator to be specifically booked by the BBC for an overseas tour – South Africa *v* England in South Africa. He started off with a commentator's dream when he was able to describe a hat trick by Tom Goddard in the first Test at Johannesburg. During the war he was captured by the Japanese at Singapore and was a prisoner of war in Siam from 1942 to 1945. But in 1946 he took up where he had left off as a member of the radio commentary team with Rex Alston and John Arlott.

Jim had played cricket for Middlesex against the Universities before the war, so with his deep, rich, authoritative voice, was well qualified for the job. He was also a cricket historian with a thorough knowledge of all the developments of the game and its players. Between us we evolved a form of TV commentary, trying hard not to speak more than necessary. Our styles were very different. Jim, factual, serious, analytical and critical, myself almost certainly too jokey, and too uncritical. I was also always eager to find extra ingredients to the actual play. To me a cricket match does not consist solely of what is taking place out in the middle. There is so much else which is part and parcel of the game – a member fast asleep – a bored blonde reading a book or some small boys playing a game of their own, oblivious of the cricket they are supposed to be watching. This meant close cooperation with our producers, Peter Dimmock and Barrie Edgar in the early days, and then Antony Craxton, Ray Lakeland, Phil Lewis and Nick Hunter. With a good producer the camera can capture so much of the 'atmosphere' of a game, and I still believe that it gives better entertainment to the viewer than just sticking to bat and ball.

In addition to commentary, Jim used to do close-of-play summaries and both on television and radio these were better than anyone else's, so good was his analysis and reading of a day's play. On television he would sometimes stop and snap his fingers and ask someone moving behind the camera to keep still. It takes a bit of guts to do this, and also breaks the train of thought. But he always seemed to be able to pick up where he had left off. I only once saw him flummoxed. When he finished his summary he used to remove his field glasses from around his neck, and place them on the table in front of him. He would then give the close-of-play score and say goodbye. He did this once at a Test at Trent Bridge where they had the giant *electric* scoreboard: 'Well, that's it then,' said Jim. 'A fine day's play – one I shall always remember. Let me just give you the close-of-play score.' So saying, he looked up at the scoreboard, only to find that it had been switched off, and there was nothing on it! As so often happens, Jim could not remember the exact score, so there was a lot of snapping of fingers, while an assistant hurriedly wrote it down on a piece of paper for him.

As I've said, he was an ideal subject for leg-pulls. In 1964 for some reason Jim had a chauffeur to drive him around. He was doing the television commentary with us at Trent Bridge, which was packed. At about twelve noon Denis Compton went to the man on the public address system and asked him to read out a note which we had written up in the box. Between overs the crowd heard: 'If Mr E. W. Swanton is listening will he please go to the back of the pavilion, where his chauffeur has left the engine of his car running.' Quite untrue of course, but I've never heard such a roar of laughter from a cricket crowd.

The year before at the Lord's Test between England and the West Indies we were told that they were electing a new

Pope in Rome. The Sacred College of Cardinals was in conclave in the Vatican, and a vast crowd was waiting in St Peter's Square to see the white puff of smoke from a chimney in the Vatican. This was the traditional method of announcing to the world that the new Pope had been elected. We were told that if this happened during our commentary, TV would immediately leave Lord's and go straight over to Rome. But before this happened, I was doing the commentary and spotted that one of the chimneys of the old Tavern had caught fire and was belching out smoke. So we quickly got one of the cameras directed on to the chimney and I announced: 'Ah, I see that Jim Swanton has just been elected Pope!' He was actually rather pleased!

One other leg-pull took place in the same year at Canterbury when we were televising the August Bank Holiday match. Colin Cowdrey, who had broken his left wrist in the Lord's Test, was one of our commentary team, and before play started we arranged everything with that arch leg-puller Peter Richardson, then captain of Kent. We knew that he would be batting and so told him that we would wave a handkerchief from our scaffolding when Jim was commentating. We had also embroiled Bill Copson, the umpire, in the plot.

When Jim had been commentating for an over or so, we waved the handkerchief. As soon as he saw the signal Peter went and had an earnest mid-wicket conversation with his partner, looking up at our commentary box. They then went and had a word with Bill Copson. He then began to walk towards our scaffolding and Antony Craxton, our producer, said to Jim in his headphones: 'What's going on Jim? Comment please on the mid-wicket conference, and what Bill Copson is doing.'

'Ah,' said Jim, 'obviously some small boys by our commentary position are playing about and putting the batsmen off. Quite rightly Bill Copson·is coming to sort things out.' But by then Bill had got about twenty yards from us, stopped, and, cupping his hands to his mouth, shouted so that all the crowd (and television viewers) could hear: 'Will you please stop that booming noise up there in the commentary box. It's putting off the batsmen. Please stop it at once.'

Colin Cowdrey, just to rub it in, shouted back to Copson: 'Sorry Bill, we couldn't quite hear. Will you repeat that please?' Copson did so, and once again we heard a cricket crowd roaring with laughter. Jim of course soon realized that his leg had been well and truly pulled, and said that Peter Richardson must be up to one of his silly tricks, and that we should get on with the game.

As you may have gathered, we had many happy days in the television commentary box, and in spite of our irreverence, I know that Jim too enjoyed his time in the box with us. Let me tell one final story at his expense – as related by Colin Ingleby-Mackenzie at the Eton Rambler dinner in 1982. Not having been present at the occasion he referred to, I am unable to vouch for its veracity! Apparently, on the first night of their honeymoon, as Jim and his wife were getting into bed, Ann's foot touched Jim's.

'God,' she said, 'your feet are cold.'

'It's all right, darling,' he replied. 'In bed you may call me Jim.'

Peter West

My other regular colleague of those days, Peter West, was a complete contrast to Jim. I suppose he can lay claim to have done more hours on television since the war than any other commentator. He has certainly been a Jack-of-all-sports, partly because the producers knew he would never let them down. He quickly learnt all the intricacies of television commentary and presentation and is the complete TV professional. Of the major sports on television he has covered cricket, rugby, tennis, hockey, rowing and field events in six Olympics. In addition he has been chairman and presenter of at least twenty games or quizzes on television and radio, including fifteen years of presenting *Come Dancing*. As if this were not enough he has written and edited books and magazines about cricket and till 1983 was the rugby correspondent of *The Times*, and does rugby commentary for radio. He also finds time to be an active chairman of a public relations firm with strong sporting contacts.

All this is proof of his versatility and capacity for hard work – something we seem to find in most commentators. But his versatility had certain disadvantages. Because he did cricket, tennis and *Come Dancing*, rugby supporters were apt to think he could not know much about their game. And so it was with other games. They most of them questioned his ability to be an expert in so many sports. Peter's answer to this would be that the producers had faith in him or they would not have continued to employ him. And, throughout his broadcasting life, working always as a freelance, he has always been in full employment as a commentator – which certainly has not happened to every freelance. He could of course add that he has always been on very good terms with his bank manager!

Peter is a very friendly person with a good sense of humour and much of our happiness in the box was due to him. These characteristics have stood him in good stead, since in cricket he has now become the presenter and interviewer as opposed to doing the commentary.

He came into cricket by pure chance. He once telephoned some copy for C. B. Fry who took a liking to him and admired his efficiency, and recommended him to the BBC. He went to the Royal Military College at Sandhurst and served in the war with the Duke of Wellington's Regiment. He was a good games player, especially at cricket. But a bad back prevented him from playing seriously, except in our many charity matches. As a commentator at cricket he combined his knowledge of the game with quick assessment, and was not afraid to give his opinion with some force. But because he knew all the players so well, he was always a kind critic and enjoyed and engineered quite a few of our pranks in the box.

Peter has not escaped the occasional unlucky choice of words. Once, when commentating at tennis, he remarked, 'Miss Stove seems to be going off the boil.' There was one occasion when he made a mess of a proposed joke. Neil Durden-Smith's wife Judith (Chalmers) had just had a baby girl which they were going to call Emma. The same week

Neil was a commentator for *Come Dancing* at one of the outside broadcasts. I suggested to Peter that he should congratulate Neil during the television broadcast with the words: 'By the way, Neil, congratulations on the birth of your daughter Emma.' To this I told Neil to reply (here comes the joke!), 'Emma-so-many-thanks.'

Not very funny, I admit, but it went for a complete Burton when on the broadcast Peter said, 'Congratulations on the birth of your daughter,' leaving out 'Emma'. In spite of this Neil replied, 'Emma-so-many-thanks,' as arranged. The poor viewers, not knowing her name, must have been very puzzled over Neil's pronunciation of 'ever'. A warning perhaps, when indulging in cross-talk, to listen carefully to your partner's cue.

Richie Benaud

For my first two years of television cricket commentary my fellow commentators included W. B. Franklin (captain and wicket-keeper of Buckinghamshire), Aidan Crawley (Oxford University, Kent and twelfth man for England against South Africa in 1929), R. C. Robertson-Glasgow (wit, raconteur and brilliant cricket writer, of Oxford University and Somerset) and Percy Fender (England and astute, big-hitting captain of Surrey). I was then joined by Robert Hudson for a short period and later by Jim Swanton who with Peter West and myself formed the regular television commentary team throughout the fifties and sixties. In 1958 Denis Compton retired from first-class cricket and became an expert summarizer, and in 1960 – rather surprisingly, as he was still captain of Australia – Richie Benaud began his long stint as a commentator, which happily still continues. He joined the *Test Match Special* team on radio in 1960 and then, when he retired from Test cricket, came to us in television.

He was always a good communicator and appreciated the importance of good public relations. When captain of Australia he started something which had never been done before and, so far as I know, has not been done since. After each day's play in a Test Match he would give a press conference for the English and Australian cricket writers. Nowadays this only happens at the end of a match. He gave good value too as he was completely candid and never evasive in his answers. He would talk about the day's play and clear up any misunderstandings about incidents or doubtful umpires' decisions. He was fair in his judgement and assessment of players on both sides. It was ideal for the press as he more or less wrote their articles for them. It was also good for Richie and Australia, because no matter how fair he would try to be, both the English and Australian press were being given an Australian point of view.

When he was over here in 1956 and 1961 he took a great interest in our television commentaries. In fact at the end of the tour he managed to arrange a crash TV course for himself at the BBC. He was a quick learner and soon learnt all about the use of cameras and the tricks of the trade in commentary.

He is possibly the best organized commentator that I know. His whole year is carefully mapped out by his wife Daphne and there is not, I suspect, a single *idle* day in his diary. If he is not working you can be sure he will be playing golf. In our winter he is at home in Australia running his public relations and sports news agency and commentating for TV on any Tests there are out there. His schedule is killing. He is up every day at dawn, dictating, writing or telexing, and after a busy day there are usually dinner parties at night. If you go to his flat for dinner the hospitality is superb, but in the background there is still the ticking of telex and tape machines.

He usually comes over to England with Daphne in May having reported on a few golf tournaments round the world at the end of the Australian cricket season. They set up office in their flat over here, and the same punishing schedule continues. But of course it's not all work and Richie is a lover of good food and wine, and is an excellent judge of both. At the end of the season, in September, he and Daphne sometimes go on a gastronomic tour of France – lunch in one place, dinner somewhere else. But in spite of all this good living he has kept his figure better than most commentators, partly because golf now plays a big part in his life. Only last year during the Edgbaston Test I met him coming in for breakfast after getting up at 6 a.m. to practise by himself for a couple of hours or so.

I have always considered Richie the best of all the post-war captains, better even than Bradman or Brearley, and he makes an ideal TV commentator. From his experience as captain he reads a game with great skill, and can usually guess which tactics will be employed or suggest which ones should be. He has confidence in his own judgement and is never afraid to give his opinion about anything – even if it differs from that of his colleagues. He has a dry sense of humour and it is a pity that television tends to discourage this.

I remember that he, Peter West and myself used to have a pact that as soon as the batsman had hit the ball we would say, 'That will be one run,' or, 'two', as the case might be, and if we could immediately say, 'That's four all the way,' it was considered a minor triumph. Richie was by far the best at this and seldom got it wrong. I used to be very bold and shout 'Four', but frequently had to make an excuse when the ball was brilliantly fielded or stopped just short of the boundary. We had a lot of laughs – usually at my expense. I was never much of a judge of a run when I played, and often, I'm afraid, ran people out.

One last example of Richie's great energy. After a full day's commentary, which in his off-duty moments includes a close study of the racecourse runners and starting prices, he will appear in front of the camera after close of play, and give a slick and accurate summary. He does it all out of his head without notes and also has to cue in various film inserts to illustrate what has happened. It is not easy to do but he does it supremely well. And one other thing you have probably noticed – even at the end of a long hot day he is immaculately dressed and must certainly qualify as the cricket commentators' nattiest dresser.

Jim Laker

In the last decade BBC Television's other main commentator on cricket, alongside Richie Benaud, has been Jim

Laker – two experts not just on reading a game, but on summing up the strengths and weaknesses of batsmen and bowlers. Since 1956 Jim has walked through life with a halo round his head shining '19 for 90'. How can you argue with a man who has performed such a feat? It must have given him the confidence and self-assurance which he undoubtedly possesses. He *is* a fine judge of cricket, knows it and sticks to his opinion. He has a completely different commentating style from anyone else I have ever heard. His voice is flat and unexciting. His 'battin' and bowlin'', spoken in his Yorkshire accent, would not be tolerable from anyone else. Who ever heard of a commentator dropping his g's? But he does, and gets away with it. He is laconic, with a shy wit and unlike most commentators avoids any frenetic excitement, no matter how sensational the happening. He is as leisurely as he was when, as a bowler, he trod slowly back to his mark, walking on his heels, looking up at the sky, before wheeling round and starting his short run up to the wicket. His commentary style is in fact ideally suited to television cricket, and with his knowledge and authority the viewers could not technically be in better hands.

His whole temperament matches the pace of his walk – placid. I remember how, after he had achieved that unbelievable 19 wickets for 90 runs in the Fourth Test against Australia at Old Trafford, I went over to the pavilion to collect Jim for a TV interview. There was a hubbub of excitement in the dressing-rooms, everyone laughing and talking at the tops of their voices. Champagne corks were popping. But Jim? He was the calmest person there, graciously accepting the many congratulations with modesty and a broad smile. I remember telling someone that instead of having created a Test record which must surely stand for all time, he looked as if he had just taken a couple of wickets in a parents' match.

He was undoubtedly the greatest of all off-spinners. Trevor Bailey once said that facing Jim was like being a rabbit caught in the headlights: petrified, stationary and instinctively knowing one was about to be slaughtered. My own personal experience of his skill was in one of those

Sunday charity matches in which I was keeping wicket. Immediately Jim came on, I noticed the difference between him and the other bowlers. I found I was taking every ball chest-high. He got bounce and spin – a result of his perfect action. I was soon to learn why he got so many of his wickets from the ball which 'went with his arm', the batsman playing for an off break and giving a catch to the wicket-keeper or first slip. To me it was impossible to spot which one was not going to turn from the off. So when a batsman left his crease to a ball which pitched about middle and off I moved across to the leg-side to effect what I thought would be a sensational leg-side stumping. Imagine my horror – and Jim's delight – when the ball beat the batsman and went for four byes *outside* the off-stump, leaving me looking a complete clot in missing a stumping by being in the wrong place.

Alan McGilvray

One or two older readers may remember someone called Jack Smith, the whispering baritone. He used to sing songs like 'Baby Face' and 'Miss Annabelle Lee' very softly at the piano during the twenties and thirties. For the past fifty years the Australian Alan McGilvray – from now on 'McGillers' – has been the whispering *commentator*. His style is utterly unique. He speaks right up against the microphone so confidentially and so quietly that even if you are sitting next to him, you cannot hear what he is saying. It is a very effective method as it gives the air of intimacy which makes the listener at home think that he is the one person to whom Alan is talking. His commentary flows freely at about the same level, his voice rarely generating excitement. His description of play is completely factual and he has always been wary of following the English style of 'colourful' commentary.

I would say he is the most unbiased commentator I have ever heard. He likes to enjoy good cricket, no matter who is winning, and has very high principles as to the conduct of players and the spirit in which the game is played. He is a fine reader of the tactics and cricketing skills and is well qualified to give his judgement. In addition to the experience gained during his fifty years of commentary, he also captained New South Wales in the Sheffield Shield in 1934–36. He succeeded Don Bradman as captain and had people like Bill O'Reilly and Jack Fingleton under his command, he himself being a useful fast medium bowler.

One other unusual feature of his commentary is that he often looks through his binoculars while commentating, the field glasses resting on the top of the microphone, his elbows on the desk in front of him. I find this a very difficult thing to do, and BBC commentators rarely do it and then only for the odd ball or two. The trouble is that although you get a fine close-up of the batsman and the stumps, if the ball is hit anywhere, it goes out of your vision. It is then very difficult to take down the binoculars, and pick up where the ball has gone.

McGillers did his first cricket commentary in 1934, and so is by far and away the longest-serving and most experienced commentator. He broadcast his two-hundredth Test at Melbourne in 1980, and received a tremendous ovation from the crowd when this fact was recorded on the giant scoreboard. He first came here to represent the Australian Broadcasting Commission in 1948 and has been here many times since. But his first Test broadcasts were done from an Australian studio when they were covering the 1934 and 1938 Test series in England with 'synthetic' commentary. McGillers and others would sit in front of a studio microphone and be fed with cables sent direct from England describing *each* ball, where it had gone, how many runs scored or how a wicket had fallen. There were certain code signs so that they were able to say, as the cable describing the second ball of an over was thrust in front of them, 'Bradman has cut that one down to third man – Leyland fields and returns over the top of the stumps to Les Ames, while they trot through for an easy single.' After some experience they could pick that up easily enough from the cable. But the difficult part was when the next cable was delayed for some reason, and to fill in they had to make up 'drinks coming out', 'a dog running across the pitch', and so on. It was all backed up by sound effects of applause, cheers or gasps for a missed catch or near thing.

I gather it all sounded very realistic and they were even still prepared to use the method in 1948, if the actual commentary being relayed from the grounds became too difficult to follow due to atmospheric interference. (In those days there was no Commonwealth cable laid to take the broadcasts.) It must, though, have been a tremendous strain on the commentators, having to improvise off the cuff, using only their knowledge of the game and their imagination. The first time this unusual system was used was in 1932 during Douglas Jardine's Bodyline tour of Australia. A French radio station in Paris used Alan Fairfax who had played for Australia in England in 1930. He gave a ball-by-ball commentary from cables sent from Australia. He must have been exhausted at the end of the day, as there is no evidence that he had any other assistant.

It must have all been good training for McGillers, who stands head and shoulders above any other Australian radio commentator. With the Sheffield Shield competition, and a regular visit each year from one of the cricketing countries, he gets plenty of practice. He has done a little television but basically has stuck faithfully to radio. I always remember a conversation he and I had with that great cricket enthusiast, Sir Robert Menzies. I have said that McGillers' commentary flows along more or less non-stop. So, I suppose, does mine. Anyway, Sir Robert told us that he enjoyed our commentaries but that he preferred so-and-so up in Brisbane, 'because he knows the value of the pause'. McGillers and I understood what he was getting at, but I'm afraid it did not have much effect on our style. Sir Robert was quite right. The commentator in question would say something like: 'He bowls.' Pause. 'Outside the off stump.' Pause. 'The batsman plays and misses.' Pause. 'It goes through to the keeper.' He would then not say anything until the next ball was bowled, leaving a long gap as the bowler walked back to his mark. Imagine me keeping silent that long!

I had got to know McGillers well on his visits to Great Britain, but as I did television exclusively until the mid-sixties, I had never worked with him until I went to Australia in 1958 for my three months' 'grace leave' with ABC. He was kindness itself in the box and a great help to me in my first attempts to give the score in the Australian way. We have since enjoyed twenty-five years of friendship in the commentary boxes of Australia, South Africa and England.

He has by now got used to our somewhat more light-hearted approach, with the jokes and the leg-pulls, and has been remarkably tolerant even when he has been a victim. I caught him beautifully two years ago at Lord's. Someone had kindly sent me a large and deliciously gooey chocolate cake for my birthday. I had cut it up into slices and was busy commentating when I heard McGillers enter the box behind me. I pointed at the cake, signalling that he should help himself to a slice. His eyes gleamed and I saw him take a large piece and pop it into his mouth.

As soon as the next ball had been bowled I immediately said, 'And now I'll ask Alan McGilvray what he thought of that last delivery.' There was a spluttering noise and an avalanche of crumbs as he desperately tried to speak with his mouth full. Ever since then he has never accepted even a biscuit or sweet in the box.

There was another occasion at Edgbaston in 1975 when he inadvertently reduced the box to complete silence for nearly twenty seconds, except for the sound of suppressed giggles. We were desperately trying to fill in time during a long period when a thunderstorm had stopped play. We were talking about the Chappell brothers and in particular the youngest one, Trevor. He had done the double in the Central Lancashire League the previous season, but we were not sure how much first-class cricket he had played for South Australia. 'Well,' I said, 'let's ask someone who should know the answer. He is sitting at the back of the box – Alan McGilvray. Alan, what about it?' I turned round and there indeed was Alan at the back of the box – but fast asleep. Everyone began to laugh and I had to make a quick decision. Should I let Alan down by saying that he was asleep, or should I pretend he had left the box? I chose the latter, although there was no real reason why he should not have been asleep – he was not on duty at the time. Anyway, I quickly said, 'I'm so sorry, but Alan must have just slipped out of the box. He was here a moment ago.'

Unfortunately Alan's subconscious mind heard his name and with a snort he suddenly woke up and said loudly, 'What's that? Does someone want me? What do you want to know?' By then that rotter Don Mosey had rushed from the box with his handkerchief stuffed into his mouth, and I was left alone with Trevor Bailey, who was having quiet hysterics to my right. It was too much for me and I began to laugh uncontrollably. There was no way in which I could speak. I covered up the microphone with my hand and for once there was complete silence from *Test Match Special*, except for some strange wheezing noises. After what seemed eternity but was in fact only about twenty seconds I apologized to the listeners and decided to come clean and explain what had happened. I must say Alan took it remarkably well but it took several minutes before we were able to return to normal.

McGillers is about five months younger than me, and will certainly be remembered – when he finally retires – as the longest-serving commentator, universally respected by his colleagues as the real professional, and with a large number of appreciative friends both in Australia and England. And I am sure that listeners everywhere would universally award him the supreme accolade of 'The man who *always* gave the score' – something I think we could all learn from him.

Charles Fortune

Someone entirely different in style from Alan McGilvray is Charles Fortune, the South African commentator, who, like Alan, is still going strong. Charles has no nickname on the air except for the occasional 'Charlie'. The natural one for him was 'Outrageous' but somehow it did not stick, possibly because it was *too* outrageous. After Alan he is the longest-serving commentator and, now in his mid-seventies, he is certainly the oldest. He was born in Corsham in Wiltshire in 1906 but later became a schoolmaster in South Africa and combined it with broadcasting on cricket, tennis and rugby football. He is still used as a summarizer for rugby. His first cricket broadcast for SABC was in 1945.

He is a natural broadcaster and is capable of describing and talking about absolutely anything.

You cannot mistake Charles. He usually wears a soft trilby hat, smokes cigarettes through a holder and never ties his tie in a knot, but folds it over rather like a stock or cravate. Somewhere, I suspect, there is a monocle hidden away in a pocket. Actually, it is not *quite* true that he never ties his tie. He does make *one* exception. When we asked him to be a member of the Test Match Broadcasters Club, we presented him with its tie but only on the strict condition that when he wore it, he would tie it properly. This he has always done, and on the first day of any Test Match, when we all have to wear it, he appears with it beautifully tied. I have never really discovered why he does not tie his ties, though I believe he has not done it for nearly fifty years, and that it is in protest against something or other.

I have always enjoyed working with him. At Newlands – the beautiful Test cricket ground at Capetown – a goods train used to pass the ground regularly at 11.50 every morning. Whenever I was on I always mentioned it, and the driver must have kept a radio in his cab, because he always gave us a hoot as we called out 'Good Morning' to him over the air.

Without wishing to belittle the other cricket commentators, I would say that Charles has always been near the top of the league for 'best educated commentator'. He is well read, has a fund of general knowledge and a good choice of words and language. If it were possible – and I hope neither of them mind – he has been the nearest thing to John Arlott in style and content. He speaks slowly and clearly and obviously relishes a *bon mot* or choice of phrase. He has always been close to the players and brings his knowledge of their personalities and lifestyle into his commentaries. Like me he looks for all those little extra somethings at a cricket match and rolls his tongue round colourful descriptions of the scene in front of him. He knows his cricket well but has often been accused of concentrating on everything except for the play going on and the score. There is a marvellous story told about him, purely apocryphal I know, but near enough to the truth to portray his style of commentary.

South Africa was batting in a Test Match against Australia at Adelaide. Charles is reported to have said, 'At the start of this over from Lindwall, South Africa are sixty-three for no wicket, and from my commentary position I can see the beautiful spire of St Peter's Cathedral silhouetted against the azure blue sky. Away to the north are the towering Lofty Mountains – magnificent in their grandeur, and making a worthy backdrop to this most lovely of grounds. In a far corner I can see a group of small boys playing their own game of cricket, using a lemonade bottle as a bat. Just below me a flock of seagulls are settled in front of the sight-screen having their afternoon tea, whilst in the George Giffen Stand the ladies make a superb picture in their gaily coloured dresses. And that brings us to the end of that over by Lindwall. South Africa are now sixty-three for three – and my scorer tells me that hat trick by Lindwall was the first of his career.' I told this story in a 'This Is Your Life' type of programme about Charles on South African Television in 1981 and he took it very well!

He is also the only cricket commentator I know who has commentated in his pants. It was very hot in our box at Johannesburg one day and when I had finished my stint at the microphone I handed over to Charles who was sitting beside me. I noticed for the first time that his trousers were hung up on a hook and there he was in his pants. I didn't give him away on the air but alas for him the Director-General of SABC was showing a V.I.P. round the various commentary positions. We had just returned listeners to the studio when the Director-General came in and said to the V.I.P., 'And now I'd like you to meet our senior cricket commentator – Charles Fortune.' Poor Charles stood up rather sheepishly in his pants and shook hands.

It will be a sad day for world cricket when Alan and Charles finally retire. They have been good friends of this country and have been able to concentrate on cricket as their number-one priority. They have been able to tour with their teams and for over thirty years each has been a regular commentator at home. There is virtually no one else to take their places as cricket specialists. Their successors will be sports broadcasters who will be expected to cover *all* sports. My own feeling is that eventually radio will follow the example of television. Their commentators will be old Test players with the accent on knowledge of cricket rather than the technique of broadcasting. In Australia the late Jim Burke was a perfectly good commentator and in South Africa Neil Adcock is a regular on SABC. So these two ex-Test players show that it *can* work. Will this happen in England?

Vic Richardson

Vic Richardson is best known for his inter-over comments and his famous cross-talk act with Arthur Gilligan. But in Australia he also did some commentary and at Adelaide in 1966 for the fourth Test against England, he was a member of the ABC commentary team with Alan McGilvray and myself. He achieved what will probably be an all-time record for a commentator. He became the first grandfather to comment on his grandson playing in a Test. It was in fact Ian Chappell's first Test Match. I was the commentator when Australia's fifth wicket fell at 383, Doug Walters having been caught by Jim Parks off David Brown for nought.

Down the steps from the George Giffen Stand emerged the youthful Ian Chappell, aged twenty-two, and I suddenly realized what a unique opportunity this offered. Vic was at the back of the box during his rest period and I signalled to him to come and take my place, although it was not his turn to do commentary. I was able to say, 'Now for the first time in any Test Match here is a grandfather to comment on the very first ball his grandson receives in Test Cricket. Come on in, Vic.' And so it happened, though for the life of me I cannot remember what happened to the first ball. At any rate Ian was not out to it, as he went on to make seventeen.

Vic was most grateful for being given the chance. He had been a fine cricketer, a hard-hitting bat and superb close fielder. He also made an inspiring leader when he captained Australia in South Africa in 1935/36, Australia winning the series 4-1. He was a great sportsman who played cricket in the right way. What he would have thought of some of the antics which go on today on the field I dread to think – especially as his grandson Ian has been concerned in quite a few of the more unsavoury incidents.

Alan Gibson

One of the earliest commentators on *Test Match Special* was Alan Gibson who did his first radio commentary for BBC in 1948. Although for many years he has been associated with the West Country, he was in fact born in Sheffield. He captained Queen's College, Oxford, at cricket and was also president of the Union. He was possibly the most intellectual, articulate and wittiest of all commentators. He had an extensive vocabulary and a strong, confident voice with a 'twinkle' in it. He held strong opinions and was perhaps too honest to please all the producers. If he thought a match boring or pointless he would say so. A commentator should not be required to over-sell an event or game. But nor should he under-sell it. He left the commentary box in the early seventies and since then has entertained readers of *The Times* with his hilarious accounts of cricket or rugby matches. He travels everywhere by train, and his adventures in getting to or from a match often fill most of his column. But he has an eye for a cricketer and an appropriate phrase for every happening on the cricket field. He was a very high-class broadcaster and his early departure was a severe loss to radio.

Alan has been credited – but wrongly so, I believe, with a remark made by a commentator during the Oval Test against New Zealand in 1969. When a fast medium bowler called Cunis came on to bowl the commentator remarked, 'This is Cunis at the Vauxhall End. Cunis – a funny sort of name. Neither one thing, nor the other.'

Norman Cuddeford

'Cudders' does not rely on broadcasting for his living. He looks on it as a hobby which takes him to big events and faraway places. It is a relaxation from his insurance business, though you would not realize it from his professional approach. He has a clear, young-sounding voice, and has the ability to speak fast but to be completely intelligible. He has done quite a bit of cricket round the counties but his strong sports are athletics and lawn tennis. In a fast race he can keep up with the best and there is a sense of zest and enjoyment in everything he does.

I suppose he will always be best remembered in broadcasting circles for his appearance on the *Today* programme. He was there to read out the sports bulletins which are normally at about 7.27 a.m. and 8.27 a.m. All the contributors to *Today* sit around a large round table with microphones positioned like the numbers on a clock. When there is an item being broadcast which has previously been recorded, there is momentary relaxation in the studio while the tape is being played. Sometimes the presenters practise their next introduction out aloud to make sure it sounds all right.

On this occasion, at about 8.24 Cudders was sitting with his script in front of him, waiting for his turn. He was concentrating and checking up on his script when he thought he heard John Timpson *rehearsing* his cue out aloud. He heard John say, 'Norman Cuddeford has been keeping an eye on the sporting scene for us. So Norman can you please bring us up to date with the score in the Test Match between Australia and England at Sydney.' Cudders thought he would join in this 'rehearsal' and to be funny said with a laugh, 'No. As a matter of fact I can't!' The result was the complete collapse of everyone in the studio, with John desperately signalling to Cudders that it was a genuine cue. Cudders, very red in the face, then had to apologize and read out his script to the listeners. That's a moment he will never forget!

Peter Cranmer

One of the most popular commentators on the Test and county circuit in the fifties and sixties was Peter Cranmer – inevitably known as 'Cranners'. He was a magnificent ath-

lete, a rugger blue at Oxford with sixteen caps for England
as a strong-running centre three-quarter. He just missed a
cricket blue at Oxford but played first-class cricket for
Warwickshire and was their captain in 1938/39, and
1946/47. He was a fine fielder, a hard hitter and a tearaway
bowler. As a commentator he was completely natural –
almost conversational. He combined his considerable knowledge of cricket with a cheerful exuberance which made him
easy on the ear, and a delightful companion to work with.

He sometimes found difficulty in the more basic skills of
broadcasting, like time-keeping and cueing over. When we
were doing three commentary matches every Saturday
afternoon, plus racing, tennis and athletics it *could* become
complicated. Remember that in those days we used to work
to a pre-arranged timetable on a cue-sheet. We would then
cue over to each other at the appropriate time, no matter
what was happening in the various matches. Nowadays the
presenter in the studio is completely in charge. He cues
over to the commentators, who wear headphones. He then
tells them when to stop, saying something like: 'Brian, go to
the end of the over, and then give the score.' On hearing
the score at the end of the over, the presenter picks up in
the studio and cues over to someone else. This is of course
a far better method as it is completely flexible, and means
that the programme can spend longer on an exciting match
with only brief coverage of dull ones.

I remember that one Saturday afternoon Cranners was at
Edgbaston and I was at Leyton. As I said, he was not too
good on his time-keeping, and cued over to me at least five
minutes later than he should have done. I couldn't resist
saying, 'Thank you, Cranners. Better Leyton than never.'
Cranners is a lovely chap who in the past few years has
been stricken with illness. But he still comes to the Tests at
Edgbaston and is as cheerful as ever. He *was* fun to work
with.

Neil Durden-Smith

One of the most versatile of commentators, who came to
the BBC after retiring from the Royal Navy and after a

spell as aide-de-camp to that very popular Governor-General of New Zealand, Lord Cobham, 'Durders' joined the BBC originally to help organize the broadcasting of the World Cup, a complicated job with such tremendous world-wide coverage. But it wasn't long before his love and knowledge of cricket gained him a seat in the commentary box.

He had played for the Combined Services and at one time was very near to taking over the captaincy of Worcester. He still is a first-class batsman, and plays most of his cricket for the Lord's Taverners, of whom he was chairman for two years. He is quietly spoken and almost gentle in his delivery. He hasn't had that little bit of luck so necessary to achieve all you want in life. I believe that more than anything he would like to be a regular member of *Test Match Special*. He has broadcast Tests, but had never gained a regular place in the team. I am afraid that first with John Arlott, and now me, broadcasting well over the retirement age, opportunities for the new commentators have been scarce. He knows his cricket inside out, and as a result possibly interjects his own opinion rather than consulting our two experts. But he's still in his very early fifties and he may well achieve his ambition, though his main occupation is his public relations business. He works for television, both BBC and ITV, and covers hockey, at which he was a class player, show jumping and Polo – not the easiest game on which to commentate. For radio he has taken over from Robert Hudson and brought a touch of the Navy to that most Military of occasions – Trooping the Colour. If you can get away with a commentary on that without incurring the wrath of a dozen or so retired colonels, then you can scale any height.

He will always be known in O.B.s as the broadcaster with the best excuse when he missed his cue during a broadcast. He was at Leicester during one of these Saturday-afternoon round-ups and the presenter cued over to him according to his cue-sheet just after the tea interval should have finished. But there was dead silence except for the distant applause from the crowd. So the presenter went over to the other commentary points for the next ten minutes or so. He then decided to try Durders again:

'. . . Are you there now, Neil? We tried ten minutes ago and couldn't raise you.' There was a slight pause, then a very out-of-breath Durders managed to blurt out, 'I am sorry. I can hardly speak. I've just run up the stairs to the box. I'm late because I've been having tea with the Bishop of Leicester.' This was of course greeted with roars of mirth by his colleagues in their commentary boxes all round the country. It was the best – and most unlikely – excuse ever heard on the air. When Durders cued over to Alan Gibson at Worcester Alan said in a sombre voice, 'I regret that there are no episcopal celebrations here.'

Pearson Surita

Pearson Surita came from Calcutta, where in addition to his cricket, he was a judge at the races. He had a benign, friendly face with a slightly surprised look on it. He spoke slowly with rather a posh accent and laughed easily with a pleasant chuckle. He knew his cricket and was most helpful to us with his knowledge of Indian names and customs.

His sense of direction was perhaps not all that it should be. On the England tour of India in 1981/82, just before close of play one day, he and Don Mosey were having an argument about which way the pitch at Eden Gardens faced. Pearson, who of course knew the ground better than most people, insisted that it faced one way; Don the other. Sitting in the studio back home I was inclined to back Don, because if Pearson was right at the time when they were broadcasting the sun was setting in the north! I have never been to India, but I am assured by those who have that it is the same there as everywhere else – it does actually set in the west. But even when he visited us in our box at Lord's the following summer, Pearson was still insistent that he was right.

Roy Lawrence

I worked with Roy Lawrence both over here and in the West Indies. He was a kind, gentle person and an excellent commentator, with a detailed knowledge of West Indian cricket. He lived in Jamaica, but during the seventies came over to Great Britain and lived in Harrogate. But when there was a change of government and things became more settled, he returned to Jamaica in 1981. His worst moment on the air must have been during the tear-gas riots at Sabina Park during Colin Cowdrey's tour of 1967/68. I was with him in the commentary box as the bottles began to be hurled on to the field. When the police used the tear-gas they miscalculated the wind and the gas was blown across our box and the press box, and after a few spluttering and gasping moments we had to give up trying to describe the scene and returned listeners to the studio. When the riot had stopped and the gas had cleared Roy made a most moving apology on behalf of West Indian cricket, especially as the trouble had been on his beloved Sabina Park. He unashamedly broke down, and it was one of the most dramatic broadcasts at which I had ever been present.

On a lighter note, he has admitted that he once opened a broadcast in 1960 with: 'Well, it's another wonderful day here at Sabina Park with the wind shining and the sun blowing gently across the ground'!

Tony Cozier

The other West Indian commentator with whom I have enjoyed working both here and in the West Indies is Tony Cozier, for whom, strangely, I have no nickname. In contrast to Roy Lawrence he is a forceful character and a lively and enthusiastic broadcaster, not afraid to speak his mind. Perhaps more than any other overseas commentator he has had to defend his country's team against criticism, given I hope in a friendly fashion, by the majority of the *T.M.S.* team. Of course, this criticism has had nothing to do with the standard of the West Indians' cricket. How could it, when they have recently proved themselves so superior to England, and are undoubtedly the outstanding team in the world of Test Cricket?

The criticism has been given because of the slow over rate of their bowlers and the excessive number of bouncers which they tend to bowl. Coming from an Englishman it must sound rather like sour grapes but I personally feel it is justified. On the other hand it is largely compensated for by the magnificent stroke play of their batsmen, and the awe-inspiring speed of their bowlers — they have no need to bowl so many bouncers.

At any rate Tony has a simple answer to all such criticism.

Look at the results, he says. The West Indian record speaks for itself. The slow over rate does admittedly rob the spectators of a considerable number of overs a day. But look at the entertainment they get watching these fast bowlers in action, and seeing so many wickets tumble quickly during a day. As for the bouncers, he says, that is entirely in the hands of the umpires, and they have the necessary powers to stop them if they think they are deliberately intimidating.

That's certainly true, but the umpires don't in fact stop them, either in England or in the West Indies. But Tony has a strong argument. The West Indies have found a type of bowling combination based on speed, which enables them to beat all the other Test-playing countries. They also draw large crowds wherever they go. So why should they change their tactics? Tony puts this case over very well in a perfectly friendly way but quite rightly feels he should defend his country.

He is a very hard worker, writes for the newspapers and travels with the West Indies team on their tours abroad. When in Great Britain he manages to play some club cricket, and on the Monday mornings regales me with his successes behind the timbers. He is an expert on all West Indian cricketers and their records which makes the following story a little less cruel than it sounds.

During the first Test Match at Queen's Park, Trinidad, on Colin Cowdrey's tour of 1967/68, rain stopped play for some time. Tony wanted to go across the ground to the press box, so I said I would 'man' the commentary box, so as to keep the studio advised about the state of the weather. It was still raining slightly when I saw Tony returning across the field about half an hour later. As he came up the steps into the commentary box I pretended that I was speaking to listeners on the air. As he entered the box I said, 'Well, those are the up-to-date statistics of the MCC team, and you know all their ages, dates of their birthdays and their exact batting and bowling figures. Ah, I see Tony Cozier has just come into the box so I'll ask him to give you exactly the same information about the West Indies players. Tony. . . .' I have rarely seen a greater look of horror on anyone's face. He sat down at the microphone and began to stammer, making frantic signals to the scorer to hand him a copy of *Wisden*. To gain time he said, 'Well Brian, I'll try to tell listeners in a moment, but perhaps you'd like to hear something about the state of the pitch, which I have just passed on my way back.'

'No, sorry Tony,' I said, 'we've just talked about it whilst you have been away. All we want – and straight away please – is the information about the West Indies statistics.'

At this point I just could not go on, he looked so miserable and desperate.

'Well, Tony, if you can't give us the details I suppose we had better return to the studio. So goodbye from us all here.'

There was a hush for a few seconds, broken only by Tony's heavy breathing. Then I told him that we had *not* been on the air. It took him quite a few minutes to recover, and looking back I realize that it really was rather a dirty trick to play on anyone, and I am always on the look-out for someone trying it on me! Anyway, Tony has, I hope, long since forgiven me, and we always look forward to welcoming him to the box whenever the West Indies visit this country.

Alan Richards

Another overseas commentator with whom I have had the pleasure of working is Alan Richards from New Zealand. He is a cheerful, friendly person and an excellent all-round commentator. He is an Auckland man and extremely versatile in his sports. He played cricket for the provincial side at Eden Park and also played soccer in the winter, and is now a director of North Shore United – a First Division club. He is also a racehorse owner and a keen follower of the Turf, both flat-racing and trotting.

So far as cricket commentary is concerned he came over here for the New Zealand tours of 1978 and 1983, and also for the Prudential World Cups of 1979 and 1983. He has been to every cricketing country where the game is played at International Cricket Conference level. Alan had an unforgettable experience in Pakistan in the mid seventies. He was a member of the Pakistan Radio commentary team for simultaneous transmission in Pakistan and to New Zealand. He followed one of the local commentators and after doing his twenty-minute stint, handed over to another Pakistani commentator. To Alan's horror the next twenty minutes were entirely in Urdu, so that his New Zealand listeners were left completely in the dark as to what was happening!

He has some mixed memories of his Test Match commentaries. His first experience as a cricket commentator coincided with New Zealand's first-ever Test victory against the West Indies in 1956, but some of his other sixty-five Tests were not so happy.

He was at the microphone at Eden Park in 1975 when a lifting ball from Peter Lever struck Ewen Chatfield. Chatfield collapsed and swallowed his tongue and would probably have died had not England's physiotherapist, Bernard Thomas, dashed out and given him the kiss of life. Alan says this was the most difficult ten minutes of commentary he has ever had to do. But an incident at Christchurch in 1980 was not much better, when West Indian Colin Croft deliberately banged into umpire Fred Goodall, causing a hostile demonstration from the incensed crowd. Alan's job was made more difficult because his commentary was being relayed to the Caribbean and he had to be very careful in what he said.

Perhaps his most unpleasant experience was at Melbourne in 1981, when, with New Zealand requiring six runs to win off the last ball, Australia's captain Greg Chappell instructed his brother Trevor to bowl an under-arm grub all along the ground. Alan – like every sportsman all over the world – was horrified at this unsporting action, so foreign to cricket. He wisely just gave the facts without expressing his opinion, and handed quickly over to his Australian colleague Ian Brayshaw and left him to say what everyone was feeling.

In soccer he was the first English-language commentator to visit China, where he has been twice to cover World Cup qualifying games. He has not found commentary there particularly easy, with Chang passing to Wong who beats Ling and then passes to Teng who heads the ball to Pu who back-heels to Gu who slips it to Ma whose shot at goal accidentally hits his colleague Ping in the back!

On his arrival in Peking in 1975 Alan was asked through an interpreter, 'Mr Richards, has New Zealand suffered badly under the imperialist English aggressors?' Alan immediately thought of the day at Eden Park in 1955 when England had bowled out New Zealand for a record low Test score of twenty-six, but decided to answer, 'No.'

Alan must be one of the only commentators in the world to describe both World Cup cricket *and* football.

Norman de Mesquita

After a long winter's lay-off commentators – like players – need some 'net' practice at the start of the season. I am usually lucky to be given my net early in May at a John Player match at Lord's, when Norman de Mesquita invites me to share the commentary with him for Radio London. It is an ideal way of beginning the broadcasting season – Radio London covers the Sunday matches from 3 p.m. till close of play, so this enables each commentator to get quite a few twenty-minute stints of commentary.

Norman is a fluent talker who, unusually for a commentator, makes no claim to have been a good games player, describing himself as a 'non-coordinator'. But he went through a far tougher and more difficult preparation by umpiring at cricket, and refereeing at soccer, when he was in the RAF and later for the Press Association. And as if that were not enough, he was an ice hockey referee for fifteen years. He is in fact an ice hockey enthusiast. He had his first skating lesson one afternoon in November 1947 after watching the Royal Wedding of Princess Elizabeth and Prince Philip. He used to sell the *Ice Hockey World* outside the stadiums, watched every ice hockey match which he could and then became qualified as a referee.

He has a good knowledge of cricket, a cheerful voice and a keen sense of humour. He believes in keeping in close touch with the players and so far as the South East clubs are concerned there is nothing which he doesn't know about the players' characters, their foibles and abilities. He is the only commentator I know who commentates and keeps the score at the same time, by the complicated method used by Bill Frindall – something I could never do. Towards the end of a John Player match he is able to make rapid calculations of how many runs are needed in how many balls – and keep describing what is happening on the field at the same time.

He has learnt never to prophesy at cricket. In one John Player match between Middlesex and Lancashire the scores were level, with five wickets in hand and plenty of overs left. He unwisely remarked that the game was as good as over and that Lancashire had won. How wrong he was. They collapsed, lost their five wickets for no more runs, and the result was a tie!

Norman has just passed the half-century and lives in Cricklewood in the same house where he was born. He has, I would say, two ambitions. Instead of staying in local radio he would dearly like to go national and ultimately become a member of the *Test Match Special* team – for whom he has already done several World Cup matches. He would also like to become a modern Stewart Macpherson, if only television or radio would give regular coverage to ice hockey. Meanwhile he keeps his hand in by commentating every year on the Harlem Globe Trotters during their annual tour of Great Britain.

Please note, by the way, that I have – almost – refrained from calling my start-of-season practice my 'Mesquita net'!

CHAPTER 8

The Changing Scene

During the sixties and seventies the pattern of outside broadcasting gradually began to change, both on television and radio, but especially the latter. In fact, except for the big ceremonial occasions and regular hardy annuals like the Opening of Parliament, Trooping the Colour, the Lord Mayor's Show, the Festival of Remembrance and the Cenotaph Service, plus of course sport, O.B.s have taken a back seat. No longer are there special O.B. features like *Saturday Night Out* or Bank Holiday visits to seaside resorts. There are no more live broadcasts from London theatres, no more regular cricket commentaries from county matches.

This of course means that would-be commentators get less and less experience and practice at what is not an easy art anyway. In fact I am always amazed how the BBC Television and Radio do such a superb job when the big occasion *does* arise, with the commentators being thrown in at the deep end.

There are several reasons for the change. For every O.B. there have to be Post Office lines from the Television Centre or Broadcasting House to the broadcasting point. Over the years these have become so expensive that an O.B. is now something of a luxury. Even more important has been the arrival of recording tape, and the resulting economy.

A reporter or commentator can now go to an event on his own with just his tape recorder. He can record his commentary with all the necessary sound effects, and come back to the studio. The cost is minimal and the tapes can quickly be edited to fit the available broadcasting time, or to eliminate mistakes or poor quality. Besides saving money it is a tremendous temptation for the producer, who can still get his 'actuality' and have the final say in the output without any of the risks involved in a 'live' O.B. It is also a great saving in manpower and therefore in costs. For a normal radio O.B. there might only be one or possibly two engineers. But to mount a television O.B. is a terrific job and for these there can be as many as thirty-five to forty people involved.

There is one other factor in the partial demise of commentary. The pace of broadcasting has increased. Programmes are more tightly planned. A lot of the leisure and relaxation has gone. The accent now is on news; short, snappy reports are the order of the day. Producers try to cram in as much as possible without lingering too long at any one event. Communications too have improved dramatically. Cables and satellites mean that the viewers and listeners can be whisked around the world at the flick of a switch. The quality is superb and the old crackles and fading have largely disappeared.

But these long distance communications are also very expensive so that brevity and concise reporting have taken the place of more colourful and long descriptive pieces. The reporter with a news sense is gradually taking over from the commentator, who anyway cannot earn a good enough living by commentary alone. That's not to say that as a breed we are starving! But even the best of the commentators have always needed to supplement their incomes by other more regular work. Raymond Glendenning wrote for the papers; Stewart Macpherson had *Twenty Questions* and *Ignorance is Bliss*; Richard Dimbleby *Down Your Way*, *Twenty Questions* and *Panorama*; David Coleman *Sportsview*, *Sportsnight* and *Grandstand*.

In the same way John Arlott could never have lived in the sort of comfort which he enjoys from his commentary pay alone. He has made far more by his writing, journalism and television commercials. There are just a few outstanding broadcasters like him who deservedly have made commentary the springboard to activities which offer bigger financial rewards. Yet when all is said and done I am willing to bet that for pure enjoyment they would all choose live commentary with its element of risk, challenge and – when successful – complete personal satisfaction.

The biggest school for commentators has undoubtedly been the Sports Department of Radio O.B.s. For many years after the war it was lorded over by Angus Mackay – a remarkable picker of talent and a strict disciplinarian who demanded – and usually got – the highest quality from his performers. His tradition has followed on under people like Cliff Morgan, Bob Burrows and Slim Wilkinson. The department has produced a large number of commentators not just for Radio but for BBC TV and ITV as well. There are very few television commentators who have learnt their trade in television only. The vast majority have had their initial schooling and experience in radio. I was one of the exceptions in cricket broadcasting, doing television commentary long before I tried it on radio. In the fifties I commentated on television for the big ceremonies like the King's funeral and the Coronation before I ever did a similar type of commentary for radio. But even so, all my groundwork was done in Radio O.B.s under the eagle eye of Lobby.

The lack of opportunity for modern commentators to get regular practice in their art is partly responsible for an interesting development. In general the voices of broadcasters have become less easily recognizable. It may also be partly due to the rather restricted 'school' in the Sports Department, where commentators are trained mainly in soccer commentary. Up to the end of the sixties most, if not all, of the commentators were quickly identifiable by the character of their voices. No one could fail to recognize Dimbleby, Snagge, Vaughan-Thomas, Glendenning, Macpherson, Arlott, Alston, Baxter, Bromley, Williams – to name only a few. For years they had had a chance to practise and develop a style of their own.

But during the last ten years or so commentary seems to have become far more stereotyped. It is slick, efficient, expert and knowledgeable, and I am sure tells the listeners just what they want to know. But it lacks variety of voice. At one time the so-called 'mid-Atlantic' accent was fashionable and made some commentators sound similar. Today perhaps it is more the style, emphasis and delivery which all tend to be of the same pattern. Whatever it is there are at least six of the modern Sports Department commentators whom I find very difficult to tell apart. Peter Jones and Gerald Williams are the only two I would guarantee to get right – and they are both Welshmen. Perhaps the English voice is becoming more uniform, with everyone sounding more alike. None of this applies to the more leisurely games like cricket, tennis and golf where the commentators on the whole still come from an older generation.

My own broadcasting career underwent an important development when in 1963 I was appointed the first-ever BBC Cricket Correspondent. I continued all my commentary (still at that time exclusively for television) but I was also partly allied to the News Department. Whereas in the past they used to read out reports of Test Matches from the tapes, now that they had their own correspondent, they decided to risk taking live reports straight from the ground into the news. They considered it a risk because a news bulletin has to be the exact length allotted to it – usually ten minutes – to the nearest second. They were naturally worried about trusting a commentator to do exactly the time they asked for, generally a minute but on occasions as little as thirty or forty seconds. This report also often had to be given whilst the commentator was already describing play on Radio 3 or, in the case of overseas matches, on some other channel. But to their admitted amazement it worked, even over the thirteen thousand miles to Australia, and it is now an everyday event.

From my first overseas tour in 1958 until I retired as a member of the staff in 1972 I was lucky enough to do seven such tours for the BBC covering MCC visits to all the Test-playing countries except India, where at that time the poor communications made live broadcasting back to Great Britain not worth the while. In addition I also commentated on two other tours not involving England. One was for ABC when Australia played the Rest of the World in 1972, and the other for SABC during South Africa's last Test series, which they played against Australia in South Africa in 1970.

This was a unique broadcasting experiment thought up by Charles Fortune, the doyen of South African broadcasters. There were four Tests which incidentally were all won by South Africa. Charles decided to have three commentators only, with no expert summarizers between the overs. There was of course himself and the visiting commentator from Australia, Alan McGilvray. So he decided to have what he called a neutral voice and kindly invited me to be the third member of the team. Instead of the usual twenty-minute stint each, we did only fifteen minutes but had to fill in between the overs. It was something original and fun to do and I believe that SABC considered it a success.

But I think that the commentator/summarizer method is still the better way. Listeners like to hear the views and judgements of an ex-Test player who knows what it's like to be out in the middle in a Test Match. Often he will have played with or against the players about whom he is talking. Furthermore, he naturally knows far more about the tactics and cricketing skills than mere 'amateurs' like myself.

Since the mid-sixties I had shared my Test Match commentaries between television and radio. Charles Max-Muller was then Head of Radio O.B.s and had been responsible for my being made BBC Cricket Correspondent in 1963. He rightly felt that with that title I should not just be used by television. So from 1965 up to 1969 I had been doing three Tests each season for television, and two for radio, with John Arlott and myself interchanging between the two. Though sorry to be away from television I was honoured to be allowed to join the ball-by-ball commentary teams of *Test Match Special*, which had been going since 1957. It was quite difficult to change one's technique from Test to Test, trying not to talk too much at one, and then having to talk non-stop at the other.

Since the war the radio commentators had included Rex Alston, Jim Swanton, John Arlott, Alan Gibson, Robert Hudson and Neil Durden-Smith. In addition there was always a visiting broadcaster from the country which was touring England. Summarizers had included Arthur Gilligan, Alf Gover, Freddie Brown and Norman Yardley. But by 1970 Rex Alston had retired and Robert Hudson had left his commentary seat for the administrative job of Head of Radio O.B.s – taking over from Charles Max-Muller. The 1970 set-up was to be chosen from John Arlott, Alan Gibson, Neil Durden-Smith and a visiting commentator, with Freddie Brown and Norman Yardley still the summarizers.

It was on my return from this enjoyable two months away in South Africa that I got the biggest shock of my broadcasting career. The first person I ran into on my return was Neil Durden-Smith. He said how sorry he was that I was no longer going to do the cricket commentary for TV. He must have been surprised by the look of shock and bewilderment on my face, because this was the first I had heard of it. I went to see Robert Hudson – my new boss – who confirmed that he had been told of the change. He said he was sorry for me but delighted for the sake of *Test Match Special* as he wanted me to become a regular member of that team. This kind invitation certainly softened the shock, because it was undoubtedly a blow to my pride.

No one likes getting the sack, especially after being at every Test Match televised during the past twenty-four years. But to make it worse I never received any official letter from TV O.B.s to advise me of their change of plans, nor in fact any word of thanks for my twenty-four years' stint. They just let me hear it on the grapevine, and still thirteen years later I have heard nothing from them! After all, I was the staff commentator who restarted television cricket commentary after the long lay-off during the war. All my fellow commentators were freelances, and between us and our producers we had had to try to evolve the technique of television cricket commentary.

Somewhat naturally I felt bitter at the time. As a result of my happy thirteen years with *Test Match Special* all that is now forgotten. But I am still sad that TV could behave in such a way. To be fair I did eventually get a personal handwritten note from Peter Dimmock, the General Manager of O.B.s. He was very kind and said that from his own personal point of view he was very sorry that I was going.

I must emphasize that I have never questioned the right of Television to get rid of me and I understood their reason for doing so. The commentary team of Peter West, Jim Swanton, Richie Benaud, Denis Compton and myself had become a happy group of friends who enjoyed our cricket and hoped that viewers did the same. It was natural that we probably gave an 'amateurish' atmosphere to the box with too many jokes and friendly asides and back-chat.

By 1970 I think BBC TV felt that they wanted a more 'professional' approach. No more jokes, no more camera shots of extraneous attractions like the member fast asleep or the bored blonde reading a book. They wanted the commentator to stick to the cricket only, and quite obviously the best people to do this would be ex-Test players. So the new regular commentary team became Richie Benaud and Jim Laker with Peter West remaining as linkman and interviewer. Denis Compton and Ted Dexter were the main summarizers, to be joined later by Mike Smith, Brian Close, Ray Illingworth, Tom Graveney and even Geoff Boycott when not playing. The two commentators have remained the same with the occasional introduction of Christopher Martin-Jenkins. After a few seasons Denis Compton decided to drop out, feeling frustrated by the restrictions put on his natural exuberance and love of a laugh.

This television team has undoubtedly become a polished, slick, knowledgeable group of experts, backed up by a formidable array of cameras and technical expertise. Their style of commentary is tailored for the viewer who knows his cricket. But there is a majority of people viewing who don't know so much about cricket and the players, and who welcome a little light relief, to balance the many static moments which are inevitable during a game of cricket. Because the television commentary sticks so religiously to the cricket at the expense of everything else, it has somehow, with its cold, technical analysis, lost some of the warmth and friendly atmosphere of our commentary box.

It is for this reason that a great number of people either write to us or tell us when we meet them that they watch the television with the television commentary turned down, and *listen* to the radio commentary. This is in itself entirely illogical and contrary to the accepted ideal of a television commentary which is 'only speak when you can add to the picture'. If a television commentator were to talk non-stop as the radio commentators inevitably have to do, he would be castigated, and told to 'put a sock in it'. And yet people *do* apparently enjoy the combination of television picture and radio commentary. And not only in this country. It has happened for some years in Australia and came to a head during the sixth Test between England and Australia at the Oval in 1981.

Just before the Test, ABC asked their viewers to ring up and say why they listened to the radio whilst watching TV. Their telephone lines were swamped. They were so impressed by the numbers who rang up, that on the second day of the Oval Test they announced that for the first two hours before lunch they would take the BBC TV pictures, but use the *T.M.S.* sound. They did not warn us about it, and the first we knew was when Trevor Bailey received a cable just before lunch. It was from a friend of his in Australia saying that he was enjoying listening to Trevor on his television set. I believe that after the match ABC organized a poll which came out five to one in favour of the experiment.

My transfer to *Test Match Special* in 1970 was the start of what have been some of the happiest years of my life. *T.M.S.* is a rather unique institution. In fact the BBC itself has called it a 'new art form'. This, I have always felt, is rather overdoing it. But it is certainly a different type of broadcasting to anything that has been done before. I have to admit that it's during these last thirteen years that it has gradually become more different, and that I must bear some of the responsibility for this. In view of the success of *T.M.S.* this may sound boastful. But in fact there is a section of listeners who disapprove of our way of broadcasting. They are, luckily for us, a minority, but we do recognize that they would prefer the old straightforward method of commentary without all the funnies and the cakes. They obviously have a case, but from the wonderful reaction which we get from so many people we feel that we are doing what the majority enjoy. On the whole – especially in these days of high postage – viewers and listeners tend only to write when they are angry or wish to complain. We are lucky that more than ninety per cent of our large post is just to say 'thank you', and encourages us to continue as we are. Again, I go all round the country in *Down Your Way*, and it is comforting and rather touching that so many people come up and say nice things about the cricket commentary. It could, though, be argued that those who dislike it would not want to approach me to tell me so.

The change in *T.M.S.* has been gradual but it is still founded on the original concept of providing the listener with an accurate, colourful, and lively description of a day's cricket, bearing in mind also that cricket *can* be dull and does need the occasional injection of fun to maintain the listeners' attention.

Our approach to the modern *T.M.S.* is quite simple. Five or six of us go to a Test Match for just the same reasons as other spectators. We go to have fun and to enjoy ourselves. Our aim is to behave naturally as a party of friends would do. Never miss a ball – but if someone receives an interesting or amusing letter, or if one of us has heard a good story during the interval, then we like to share it with the listeners. I think the word 'naturally' is important. It means to be ourselves in front of the microphone and not to try to follow a stereotyped pattern. If there *are* strengths in *T.M.S.* they are the complete contrasts in personality of all the commentators. We are totally different in voice and character and often in opinions too. One of the amazing things is that over a span of thirty-seven years I have never had a quarrel nor seen one in the box. It's basically due to our mutual love of cricket and the way in which we all believe that cricket should be fun. It is something to savour and enjoy. The more I commentate the less I care who wins, though of course deep down it is always nice if it is England that wins. But basically I hope just to see some good cricket no matter which side produces it.

The conditions under which we work are not ideal, being often too cramped, too crowded and too hot. One would expect this to make the commentators niggly and touchy but somehow we never seem to mind. Our boxes are far

better than they used to be. Trent Bridge is the best sited –
suspended below the Pavilion balcony right behind the
bowler's arm, about twenty feet above the ground. Our new
box at the Oval is comfortable and also beautifully placed
behind the bowler, but is possibly a shade too high. Lord's
is equally comfortable but for a Test Match we are normally
looking over mid-off or fine leg. But it gives a magnificent
view of the ground. Headingley is long and narrow, and is
situated under the roof of the Rugby League stand. It gives
a good view down the wicket but we get no sight of the sky
which makes it a rather gloomy place in which to work.
Edgbaston is well situated but the box is square with a
narrow front with only room for three of us to sit – including
Bill Frindall, who inevitably takes up a lot of space with his
score-sheets, stopwatches and reference books. In the ideal
box five of us can sit in a row which allows for the commentator, the summarizer, Bill Frindall, the next commentator and anyone who has popped into the box for an
interview.

Undoubtedly our worst box is at Old Trafford: small,
hot, no space for coats or briefcases, and not even behind
the bowler's arm. I hope that before I finally retire, the
plans for a whole new complex of stand, commentary and
press boxes and even an hotel, will have borne fruit.

I suppose one of the features of our *T.M.S.* boxes is their
complete informality. Sometimes journalists spend a day
with us to write a behind-the-scenes story, and I know that
they are all surprised by the apparently casual way in which
we all behave. They comment on the lack of tension or strain
and the many asides, jokes and leg-pulls which take place
throughout a long, hot day.

But behind all this apparent casualness there is an innate
sense of discipline without which the whole structure would
collapse. We are all now experienced broadcasters for whom
the microphone causes no terror. There are certain automatic rules such as microphone technique, timing, and
punctuality either when it is one's turn to take over, or to
hand over to someone else. What success we have in this
mixture of professionalism and easy-going behaviour is
largely due to Peter Baxter, an amicable producer, who rides

us all on a light rein. He must sometimes cringe when we slightly overstep the mark but on the whole we try hard to keep a balance between being too friendly and too boringly orthodox.

As I have said, we are all very different in character, so naturally we all have different ways of spending the day at a Test, when not actually commentating. I have always made it a habit to arrive at the box at least an hour before play is due to start. The producer, Bill Frindall and Don Mosey are usually there before me. I start by opening all my letters in case there is anything which needs answering over the air. There are generally hundreds of them in the box put into neat little piles. You can just imagine the mess after they have all been opened, with empty envelopes all over the place or hopefully in our tin waste-paper basket. Each one of us tries to answer the more personal letters. Some we answer over the air, especially in our 'Listeners' Letters' spot during the lunch interval on every Monday of the Tests. But inevitably the large majority have to be acknowledged later on by Peter Baxter on behalf of the BBC. This is not very satisfactory but there is really no alternative. There is just not the time to answer the many queries we get about players, records and laws and requests to pick a best ever world XI, etc. That is why we implore people not to send valuable photos, old newspaper cuttings or autograph books through the post. There is always the danger of their getting lost in the chaos.

In addition to the letters there are the parcels to attend to, consisting of sweets, home-made cakes, bottles or other unexpected things. We quite often get tooth brushes from dentists who are worried by our eating so many sweets. On one occasion for some reason Greg Chappell lay on his back when a wicket fell and waggled his legs in the air. I said it looked like my Yorkshire terrier, Mini, who used to lie down to rub the eczema on her back. A day or two later I received some powder from a chemical firm, and even two letters from Australia offering me advice.

The most touching present I received was during that exciting Headingley Test in 1981. Fred Trueman and I have always talked about our dogs. He has a giant Old English

Sheepdog called William who once came up to our commentary box at Headingley and started to eat some of Bill Frindall's records. On this day I had checked up on William, and Fred then asked me about Mini. I replied that I was a bit worried about her because my wife was on holiday in Jersey and I was away at the Test. This meant that we had had to put her in one of those dog hotels for a fortnight, and I explained that I didn't know what her reaction would be. I said that you cannot tell a dog that it's only going to be a short stay and that Mini might think she was being left there for ever – never to see us again. I thought no more about it until an hour later there was a knock on the commentary-box door and there standing outside was a man with two dozen red carnations addressed to me. Attached to them was a note which said: 'It's all right. I know you are coming back for me. All well here – love Mini.' I must say I nearly blubbed, it was so sweet and kind of the person who had sent the flowers. I discovered it was a friendly florist in Hounslow who had heard the broadcast, rung up a florist in Leeds and asked him to take the flowers to Headingley. I really was touched. It made me realize what a close and friendly contact we have with our listeners.

There was, however, a sad ending to the story. I never saw Mini again. My wife collected her from the kennels and her condition was not too good. She was aged twelve and a half and had been blind in one eye for some time. Now she went completely blind in the course of a few weeks which she spent at our holiday home in Swanage. We thought it kinder to ask the vet to send her to that 'kennel in the skies' where she could chase squirrels to her heart's content.

However, I've digressed from what happens after I've opened my letters! There are then several things to do. First, a study of the duty roster which Peter Baxter will have pinned up to the wall. We each do twenty minutes' commentary every hour plus other pleasant chores like answering listeners' letters, taking part in 'Call the Commentator' – a telephone feature we have every Friday lunchtime, or our interview spot with a celebrity on Saturdays. This is great fun to do and we ask well-known people who love cricket to come and spend the day in the box with

us. They need not be players but they are always keen
watchers, who have achieved their fame in some other field.
Most of them come from the entertainment world. Ben
Travers, Brian Rix, Leslie Thomas, Tim Rice, Patrick
Moore, John Alderton, Ian Wallace, Robin Bailey, Billy
Wright are just a few of those who have honoured us with
their presence in the box.

You will notice that I have put Ben Travers first on the
list. He was one of the earliest celebrities we interviewed –
during the Lord's Test against West Indies in 1980 – and
there was a tremendous reaction to his broadcast. He was
then aged ninety-four and without turning a hair he climbed
the steps to our box on the top balcony of the pavilion. We
gave him a glass of champagne and when we had finished
our lunchtime summary we started our interview with him.
I say 'our' because John Arlott and Trevor Bailey were there
too. But after I had put my first question, all we had to do
was to sit back and listen for a magical thirty minutes. It
was like winding up a clock. He reminisced about players
and matches he had seen. Without a note he quoted detailed
scores starting with the Oval Test in 1896 when he saw W.
G. Grace make 24, the 1902 Test also at the Oval where he
watched G. L. Jessop's famous innings of 104 when England won by one wicket, and so on up to modern times. It
was a fantastic performance delivered with wit, humility
and a deep love and enthusiasm for cricket. What's more he
could have gone on, but we had to stop him so as not to
miss the first ball after lunch. There was a happy and a sad
follow-up to the broadcast. Luckily there was a publisher
listening who immediately got Ben to start writing a book
based on his talk with us. Ben completed it by November
and sent it to me to check. Except for one or two unimport-
ant figures it was perfect and was to be published under the
title of *94 Not Out*. The sad part was that Ben died before
Christmas, so the book became *94 Retired* – and is on my
book shelf as a delightful reminder of a gentle, witty, lov-
able man, who amazed us all that afternoon at Lord's.

But back to the commentary box with about half an hour
or so before play is due to start. I use this time to check up
about any overnight news of the two teams and try to see

the groundsman for any information about the pitch. I usually also find time to pop in and say good morning to the umpires. If one of them is Dickie Bird I tell him that the weather forecast is bad and that there will undoubtedly be some awkward and unpopular decisions to make about the light later in the day. This gets him thoroughly worried. But as he is at his happiest when the cares of the world are on his shoulders, I feel I have done some good.

If there are a few minutes left before start of play I will probably challenge Don Mosey to the first word game of the day. This is something I learnt before the war in the office of our family coffee business. I knew Don flattered himself on the use and derivation of words so I introduced the game to him a few years ago, and we've played it ever since. We play it during intervals or sometimes when we are both resting between commentary periods. We get lots of letters asking us how it is played, and after several failures by me to explain it properly, I asked Don to devise an understandable explanation. This is it.

All that is required for the word game is two people, each with pencil and paper. *Each* draws a plan of twenty-five squares, thus:

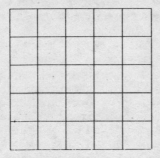

Player A says a letter – any letter of the alphabet – and *both* players place that letter in any square of their choice on the plan. Player B then chooses a letter and again *both* players write the letter into their plan. The idea is to build up words across and down the plan. Carry on giving letters in turn until twenty-four of the twenty-five squares are filled on both plans. The final square is then filled using *any* letter of each individual player's choice. Score ten for a five-letter word, five for a four-letter word, one for a three-letter word.

Any score over eighty is very, very good – over seventy very good, over sixty good, and over fifty fair. It's actually very skilful with lots of ploys such as slipping in an x, z or q to embarrass your opponent. Try it sometime – but to save arguments, have a dictionary handy.

During the day I usually stay in the box for most of the time. Some go out for a breather or a gossip with friends, others who may be writing for a paper wander off to the press box. But somehow I like to stay at the scene of action in case I miss some vital piece of play. The sponsors kindly provide us with lunch boxes, though on occasions we go for a picnic with family or friends or to one of the many boxes or tents which are features of the modern Test ground. It all adds up to a marvellously relaxing day, doing something one enjoys in the company of friends. How lucky I have been to have had such convivial and compatible colleagues, and I am grateful to them all for the way they have put up with my pranks and puns. Here they are now in alphabetical batting order.

CHAPTER 9

Test Match Special

John Arlott

John Arlott has done more to spread the gospel of cricket than any man alive. For thirty-four years his rich, gruff, Hampshire burr spanned the world. He took cricket into palaces, mansions, cottages, crofts, mud huts and, for all I know, igloos. He rightly became the voice of cricket and more imitated than any other commentator. Although he started his working life as a clerk in a mental hospital, followed by nine years in the police where he rose to Detective-Sergeant, he was basically a poet. He could do naturally what we lesser mortals had to work at – paint pictures with words. The sound of his voice alone conjured up visions of white flannels on green grass, and the smell of bat oil and new-mown grass. But his powers of description with the ever-apt phrase enabled the listener to 'see' the scene he was describing. He always tried to imagine that he was talking to a blind person and coloured his commentary accordingly. A perfect example of this was the way he once described the run-up to the wicket of the Pakistani Asif Masood. (Bill Frindall says I once called him Massive Ahsood!) He used to run with knees bent and John portrayed him with the words: 'He reminds me of Groucho Marx chasing a pretty waitress.'

One of the classic commentaries of all time was his hilarious description of the Lord's ground staff removing the covers off the square at Lord's. They took at least twenty minutes and John never missed a trick, covering every detail of what was going on. He also gave a very fine word picture of the streaker at Lord's in 1975. I know if I had been doing it I should have gone too far – 'two balls going down the pitch at the same time' – that sort of thing. But John struck exactly the right note.

He also had the enviable gift of being able to produce the apt witty comment on the spur of the moment. When he was with the MCC in South Africa the MCC captain, George Mann, was clean bowled by the slow left arm South African bowler 'Tufty' Mann. It was an unplayable ball, pitching on the leg stump and taking the off-bail. Without a moment's hesitation John said: 'Mann's inhumanity to Mann'!

He had always adored cricket and with his retentive memory soon became one of the great cricket historians. How good he was as a player I am never quite sure. But he did travel round with the Hampshire team before the war, and once at Worcester actually fielded as twelfth man for them in a county match. He was also a great listener and throughout his career cultivated the company of the county cricketers all over England – wherever he was commentating. He was not afraid to ask, and so learned much about the technique and skills of the game.

He also made many friends among the first-class cricketers and this had a happy sequel when they elected him President of the Cricketers' Association. This was a tribute and an honour and it is an office he still holds in spite of his retirement from broadcasting cricket.

We all have to have our piece of luck and his chance came in 1946 when India was touring England – the first tourists since the war. After leaving the police John had become a poetry producer for the Far Eastern Service and they selected him to follow the Indians round the country, in order to send nightly reports on the matches back to India. It was soon obvious that cricket had made a find and Lobby chose him to commentate along with Rex Alston and Jim Swanton. From then until he retired he was a member of the radio commentary team at every Test played in this country.

He was a home-lover and very much a family man so he did not tour with MCC as much as Rex Alston or, later on, myself, Christopher Martin-Jenkins and Don Mosey. In fact he paid just one visit each to the three main cricketing countries, Australia, South Africa and the West Indies.

He is an emotional, kind and compassionate man, not

ashamed to cry if he is affected that way – and incidentally he has had more than his fair share of personal tragedy. He is also witty, much enjoys conversation and can tell a funny story very well. This he usually did before play started after he had recovered from his exertions of climbing up to the commentary box. He always arrived hopelessly out of breath and more often than not mopping his brow with his handkerchief. He loathed the heat and several of us have suffered rheumatic pains in the back through his insistence on having the commentary-box door open, so as to produce a through draught.

His commentary was in the Lobby mould, describing the action until the ball was dead and then adding a piece of 'colour' until the next ball was bowled. In the same way that Neville Cardus had largely created the characters of those old Yorkshire and Lancashire professionals, so John built up the physical appearance of the cricketers – deep-chested, raw-boned, broad-shouldered were frequent adjectives. He would be fascinated by trousers too tight or shirts billowing in the breeze. The umpires in their funny hats and caps were easy game for him. But he never restricted himself to just the cricket. Like I do, he saw a game of cricket as something more than whether the ball was doing this or that. He would comment on the action going on all round the ground with a slight penchant for the pigeons feeding in the outfield. It was wonderful stuff and brought the cricket match alive.

But of course broadcasting cricket was only part of his life, albeit a very important part. He is a man of many talents and is an expert on books, wine, aquatints and glass. To visit his home is like going to a very hospitable museum. In his spare time he has amassed a wonderful collection of all those things he knows about and loves. His main hobby is drinking wine but over the years he has put more back into his cellar, than he and his friends have drunk. And that is saying a lot! I have not been to his new home at Alderney but in Alresford he made use of the old cellars of the one-time pub in which he lived. It was full of every type of wine from the old, rare and priceless to the sort which you or I would keep for a very special party. If you were his guest he would remember what was your favourite wine and there would be a bottle waiting for you in front of your place at table. It's no secret that in the commentary box we do have the occasional glass of champagne or wine which so many kind people send to us. In the old days this would have been unthinkable. In fact when I first joined *Test Match Special* I had never had any such refreshment during broadcasting hours. But John gradually introduced the idea of taking a little red wine with his lunch, and then somehow lunch used to get earlier and earlier! So that is just one of the legacies which he left behind him, and now the occasional popping of a cork in the background is usually a sign of lunch or close of play approaching.

John's cricket library was one of the largest and best private collections in the world. I say 'was', because before moving to Alderney he had to get rid of a lot of his books, only keeping the rarest and best. And in addition to cricket he had valuable first editions on other subjects.

Besides being such an expert collector John was, and still is, a prolific writer, whether reporting cricket or commenting on wine for the *Guardian* or writing on average one or two books every year. It is also the accolade for any book on cricket to have a foreword by John Arlott. He must have written hundreds. It always amazed me how he could maintain this output and still find the time and energy to commentate. For many years he did his full stint of commentating and then at close of play went off to write his piece for the *Guardian*. But in the last five years or so he used only to do three commentary periods and finished by three o'clock, so that he could go off to the press box to write. This would be enough for most men. But on Sundays he shared the BBC 2 Television commentary with Jim Laker on the John Player League. This would often mean travelling a hundred miles or more from the Test Match, and having to be back fresh for *Test Match Special* on Monday. One thing he told me once surprised me. He always took the first stint on BBC 2 from 2.00 to 3.00 p.m. Then he would do the first stint after tea, from about 4.30 to 5.30 p.m. He would then go home or back to wherever the Test Match was. This meant that he had never actually seen the finish of any of the John Player matches on which he had been commentating.

At the beginning of the 1980 season John announced that it was to be his last as a Test Match commentator – I remembered he had commentated on *every* Test played in England from 1946 onwards. He explained, 'I'm going while people are still asking me *why* I'm going rather than thinking, "why doesn't he go?"' A salutary lesson for all of us – especially for me at my time of life! In other words, although *he* didn't say so, he was going out at the top. The result was a series of dinners and presentations which went on non-stop throughout the summer – everyone wanted to give him a farewell dinner – and they did! How he stood up to it I don't know but somehow he arrived fit and well for what would be his last day – the fifth day of the Centenary Test at Lord's.

Some unwise radio reporter tried to interview him as he arrived puffing as usual at the top of the stairs. Whilst he opened the morning session there were cameramen perched in dangerous positions filming him through the window of the commentary box. There were film lights inside the box, and rows of champagne bottles sent by admirers. It was a unique day for a unique person. We couldn't really believe it all in the box – after 3.00 p.m. there would be no more John Arlott on *Test Match Special*. He got through the morning session in his usual good form, in between opening cables and letters, and celebrating in the way he knew best. We were all dreading his final twenty-minute stint, which was due to start at 2.30 p.m.

We all gathered in the box – it was packed – no one wanting to miss this historic moment in broadcasting history. The clock moved up towards ten to three and as he started what was to be his last over, we all expected him to begin a series of thank yous and farewells to the listeners. But no such thing happened. He finished the over without one single mention of his departure and then when the last ball had been bowled calmly said, 'And after Trevor Bailey it will be Christopher Martin-Jenkins.' There was a second or two's silence and then we all stood up and clapped. John got up and slowly left the box as Alan Curtis announced to the crowd over the public address system, 'Ladies and Gentlemen! John Arlott has just completed what will be his last ever Test Match commentary for the BBC.' The reaction was wonderful. The crowd applauded, the Australians and the two England batsmen turned round and clapped, and the members on the top balcony applauded and clapped John on the back as he threaded his way through them to disappear from sight. It was a dramatic and heart-rending display by the cricket world at the Headquarters of Cricket saying goodbye to an old friend who had been their favourite commentator for thirty-four years. What a triumph and what an exit. John's timing as ever had been impeccable. And a final accolade. At the end of the season MCC made him an Honorary Life Member – and no cricketer could wish for better than that.

Now John has retired to his lovely house in the Channel Isles where he writes and drinks with the many friends who go over there to visit him. He makes the occasional foray to the mainland for broadcasts, interviews or television commercials. He still writes on wine for the *Guardian*. And for the first time ever he has been able to listen in 1981 and 1982 to the *Test Match Special* which he did so much to create. We miss him tremendously for his friendship and convivial companionship. The programme misses him too for his expertise, wit and unique style of commentating. He sends us messages occasionally, but I doubt if he will ever go to see another Test. I suspect too that as he listens he must sometimes feel that Johnston has gone too far with one of his appalling puns or schoolboyish leg-pulls. If he does think so, I hope he will forgive me. Because we both in our different ways love cricket. And he can console himself that – unlike me – he never in all his cricketing life made a gaffe.

Trevor Bailey

'The Boil' is the longest-serving member of the present *T.M.S.* team, having made his first broadcast in 1965. For a change, I am not responsible for his nickname. He acquired it when playing football for Leytonstone with his great friend and fellow Essex player Doug Insole. The crowd was largely made up of cockneys and they used to encourage him with shouts of 'Come on, Boiley' – hence The Boil.

For eighteen years he has been one of our 'experts' in the box, and no one could be more qualified to that title. Captain of Dulwich College, Cambridge blue (1947, 1948), Secretary and Captain of Essex, sixty-one Tests for England, achieving the rare double of 2,290 runs and 132 wickets. In addition he took thirty-two catches and was one of the finest all-rounders who ever played for England. Most people will remember him for his many back-to-the-wall defensive innings, and his famous forward defensive stroke – head well over the ball, left hand leading, left foot towards the pitch of the ball, and the bat as straight as a Roman road. He liked winning but even more he loathed to lose and saved England on many occasions, the one which most people remember being the stand between him and Willie Watson at Lord's in 1953 against Australia.

So in addition to 'The Boil' he was also known as 'Barnacle' – something which sticks and is very difficult to remove. Ironically for one who seldom played it (except for Essex) The Boil now lives in a road called The *Drive* at Westcliff, the Essex seaside town where he was born. But to prove that he *could* hit when the incentive was there, he once scored a six in a Test Match at Brisbane, when a sponsor offered £100 to anyone who did so.

He has become a really professional broadcaster and is one hundred per cent reliable. He can fill in at a moment's notice, keep talking when nothing is happening, and is always ready to rescue a commentator when, as it has occasionally happened, he is incapable of speech because of laughter. The Boil's voice has a slightly nasal drawl with a chuckle never far away. He can be sarcastic but always does his best to be on the players' side. He knows what it's like out there in the middle. But he is a severe critic of bad tactics, bad behaviour and bad cricket. He was always a shrewd tactician with an inside knowledge of his opponents' weaknesses. Had he not broken his contract with the MCC by writing a book about Len Hutton's tour of the West

Indies in 1953/54, he must surely have been considered as Len's successor. Anyhow he speaks his mind about what he thinks are captains' mistakes, and will always deplore a player reacting badly to an umpire's decision, or gesticulating or swearing at an opponent. This is not to say that he himself was not above a bit of gamesmanship, which is very different to cheating. He might on occasion find a convenient fly in his eye just as Keith Miller was about to deliver the ball. Or he would have no hesitation in bowling down the legside as he did to save the game at Headingley against Australia in 1953. He himself has defined bad cricket as 'a night watchman trying to hit a six, a seam bowler who fails to bowl a reasonable line and length, or a very late call which leaves the other batsman stranded in the middle of the pitch. . . .'

His delivery is often staccato and has given him yet another nickname in the box – Mr Jingle. He will say, 'Fine bowler. Good line and length – moves it either way – never tires – good cricketer – like him on my side.' He also, like all of us, has his favourite adjective or adverb. His is 'literally', and he has been logged as saying, 'His tail is literally up'; '. . . it's a tense moment for Parker who is literally fighting for a place on an overcrowded plane to India'; 'Tavare has literally dropped anchor.'

On a tour or in the box he is a splendid companion, who enjoys a party more than most. He has a delightful, slightly cynical sense of humour and sometimes in triumph comes out with an even worse pun than any of mine. He is also a good feed for some of the jokes we make in the box. I remember once asking him, 'What is a Frenchman who gets shot out of a cannon called?' He repeated the question in full as every music-hall straight man always did: 'I don't know, what *is* . . . etc.' I was then able to answer: 'Napoleon Blownaparte', at which he broke with tradition and laughed. He is a joy to work with because you know he will never let you down or be lost for something to say. His broadcasting is like his batting – safe, reliable, unhurried, provocative at times, and gives the listener a sense of security. With him in the box we get the feeling that we cannot lose.

Peter Baxter

People often find it strange that a cricket commentary needs a producer. After all, they say, the game is being played out in the middle and there is nothing that he can do about it. He cannot make it more exciting nor faster-moving. The commentator can only describe what he sees. This is all true enough but of course a cricket producer is producing the *broadcast*, and at the same time directing the commentators.

The producing starts many months before a Test series, just as a film producer has a year or more of planning before a film actually starts to be made. So 'Backers', as we call Peter, has a very busy winter, not only planning the summer's cricket but in the last few years also travelling with the England team on their tours abroad to produce the commentaries relayed back to us at home. It's probably easier to list the things which he has to do before even a single word of commentary is uttered into the microphone.

Firstly, he is responsible for advising the Head of Outside Broadcasts in negotiations with the cricketing authorities over contracts for the transmission of Tests.

Secondly, he has to see that Post Office lines are booked for the various grounds and is also ultimately responsible for the care, maintenance or rebuilding of our commentary boxes.

Thirdly, he must book the commentators and summarizers well in advance and liaise with his engineering colleagues to book the engineers and technical facilities for each Test. Incidentally, he is also responsible for trying to find new commentators, and testing those whom he thinks might be suitable.

He must then check with the Controllers of Radio 3, Radio 2 and the News Department the exact time of the broadcasts, so that they can slot them into their programmes. Radio 3 takes *Test Match Special* right through the day, starting fifteen minutes before play on the first day, and five minutes before on the other four. There are then the lunch, tea and close-of-play summaries to be checked for length of time.

Radio 2 needs one-minute reports in its various news and sports bulletins and News want *their* summaries for the Radio 4 one o'clock and six o'clock news.

In addition, there are certain regular features to organize and pre-record where necessary. During the lunch interval on Thursdays of a Test there is a twenty-minute feature called 'The Great Match'. This looks back with recordings on a past Test Match at the ground from where the commentary is coming. On Fridays there is a live spot called 'Call the Commentators' which is a phone-in, and the producer, during commentary on the Friday morning, must select and write out the questions that listeners have asked on the telephone. There are usually far too many to deal with, so the producer makes as varied a selection of the subjects as possible.

Saturday lunchtime sees 'A View from the Boundary' when a well-known personality in any walk of life comes up to our box to talk about himself and cricket. The qualifications are that he should love cricket, either playing it or just watching, but he is only very rarely a first-class cricketer. One exception to this was Jack Fingleton who at Old Trafford in 1980 gave us a marvellous hour, because rain extended the lunch interval. As I mentioned before, most of our 'victims' come from the entertainment world which has always had such a close affinity with cricket.

Monday lunchtime is 'Listeners' Letters' where three of us try to answer as many of our hundreds of letters as possible in about twenty-five minutes. Tuesday is actually free of any lunchtime commitment, so the producer can at least eat his lunch in peace.

When the Test Match itself starts, Backers changes from producer to director, and nowadays is always in charge of the commentary box. Previously the producer used to sit in a studio in the bowels of Broadcasting House and conduct the broadcasts from there, being in immediate contact with an assistant in the commentary box, who would pass on instructions and comments to the commentators. But nowadays the position is reversed. Backers has an assistant in the studio to make the opening and closing announcements, play records if necessary because of rain, and read out the lunch and the county cricket scores.

Backers will arrive at the box at least an hour and a half before play. He will make out the commentators' roster detailing the times of our twenty-minute stints. He will arrange to share out the reporting duties for Radios 2 and 4, which come from a smaller box adjoining the main one. His biggest job is usually to sort out the large amount of mail and parcels and put them into neat piles. He will also make sure that morning coffee will be available when the commentators arrive.

Once play starts he is busy listening to the commentary, advising us with written cards when to welcome World Service or anyone else joining us, or reminding the commentator to give the score more often. As I have said, we are a varied lot of extroverts, and he has to try to control us without affecting the various styles and personalities. He does what is a very difficult task with a delicate and tactful touch. Whenever we go over the top he will calmly do his best to restore normality, and succeeds where someone with a more forceful approach might not.

He is a very friendly character with a great sense of humour, and is, perhaps luckily for us, an inveterate giggler. He started his broadcasting life with the British Forces Broadcasting Service in Aden in 1965, then after four months joined BBC Outside Broadcasts. He took over cricket in 1973 and, presumably because his boss thought he was not working hard enough, he was also put in charge of rugby in 1978. Except for motor racing he has worked on every type of sport and is even called in to read the racing results. He has gradually over the past few years begun to do cricket reports and some commentary from county matches, and on the tours overseas now does regular reports and interviews. He does these especially well because he is on friendly terms with all the cricketers and administrators. This is very important in order to get interviews in a hurry at close of play, or even to persuade a player who has achieved something special to come up to the box during play.

As I write there is no BBC Cricket Correspondent in

succession to myself and Christopher Martin-Jenkins. This means that during both the winter and summer Backers has often to do reports on meetings of the Test and County Cricket Board and other similar bodies and interviews for the various news and sports bulletins. I think that *Test Match Special* and the BBC are lucky to have Backers, with his vast work-rate and friendly efficiency.

Just one story which happened at Edgbaston in 1982. On the Wednesday before the Test I had recorded a *Down Your Way* programme in Worcester. During it I had interviewed a character who kept a fish and chips shop and whose nickname was 'Honky' Fletcher. As a small boy he used to deliver bread on a bicycle, and because he had no horn, whenever he went round a corner, or wanted to pass someone he used to shout, 'Honk, Honk!' – hence the nickname Honky. I was telling Backers about him one morning before play started, explaining how he used to go 'Honk, honk!' There was quite a crowd about, and when I had finished a man came up and said, 'Excuse me, Mr Johnston, I could not help hearing what you said. Some relatives of mine have just flown off to Hong Kong and as I heard you talking about it, I wonder if you could tell me what sort of place it is'!

Henry Blofeld

I have said that we are all different in the commentary box, and no one is more different than Blowers. In appearance he looks rather like a mad professor, with his horn-rimmed spectacles and long flowing hair. He normally speaks extremely fast, and this is reflected in his broadcasting. His style has been described as 'frenetic', and his voice certainly becomes excitable whenever the play warrants it. But there is a sense of tremendous enthusiasm in all that he says, and the box is never dull when he is on the air.

His descriptions of play are blended with a collection of non sequiturs depending on what his particular fancy is at the moment. Sometimes he is 'bus happy', sometimes it is pigeons or any bird he can see, and he also has a penchant for butterflies.

In 1982 at the Oval there was a helicopter rally somewhere, and he caught 'helicopteritis'. They *were* particularly tempting as they were flying from west to east over the Thames at the Vauxhall End, and he soon got into double figures totting up their runs. And of course at Old Trafford the trains passing through Warwick Road Station are an irresistible temptation. His 'busitis' was at its best (or worst!) one day at Lord's when he religiously reported every bus passing the Nursery End in Wellington Road: 'X— comes up to bowl and the ball is played quietly to mid-off as a bus comes into sight. And as Y— walks back to his mark I can see another red bus, followed by two more. . . .' And so it went on. He has such a thing about buses that at the Oval in 1982 he said, 'Here comes a *good-looking* bus!'

For a countryman he is not too sure of his birds, though he usually gets the pigeons and seagulls right. But, as a listener pointed out in a letter, Henry should know that they are not pecking the outfield for *worms*. I suppose his classic was at Headingley two years ago, when he claimed to spot a butterfly *walking* across the pitch! I would like to add that he said that it had a slight limp, but he didn't go that far. I suppose he creates more amusement and giggles among ourselves in the box than any other commentator. But he takes our gentle chaffing extremely well and proceeds unruffled to describe the play, which he does with professional accuracy. Not surprising really, because he himself briefly played first-class cricket, and for the last ten years or so has travelled round the cricketing world commentating, reporting and writing on all the Test Matches wherever they are played during the winter.

As a young boy he went to Sunningdale Preparatory School, where the headmaster was a friend of mine. He soon reported to me that he had a brilliant wicket-keeper called Blofeld in his first eleven. He was by far the best the school had ever had and played for four years in the eleven. From there Blowers went to Eton where he got into the first eleven at the age of fifteen, a very rare feat in such a big school. In 1957 – his third and last year – he was appointed captain. Everyone who went to play against the school came away praising the ability of Blowers behind the stumps. Here – in the opinion of Ben Barnett, the old Australian wicket-keeper – was an England player of the future. But sadly one day just before the Eton and Harrow match, he was involved in a terrible accident. He was having a bicycle race against his friend and vice-captain Edward Lane Fox, from Agars Plough to Upper Club – two playing fields at Eton. They were separated by the road to Datchet, and as Blowers – in the lead – cycled across it, he struck a Women's Institute bus and was flung for yards down the road. He suffered appalling head injuries, and so could not play in the match at Lord's, and his life was in the balance for some time. But somehow he made a miraculous recovery and in 1959 went on to win a cricket blue at Cambridge as a batsman. He has played good class club cricket since then and can always be proud that he kept wicket for his native Norfolk at the age of sixteen. He could also boast – but I have never heard him do so – that he was one of only three schoolboys to make a hundred at Lord's against the Combined Services. The other two were Peter May and Colin Cowdrey. So he was in good company. And he made it a double at Lord's, when in 1959 he made 138 for Cambridge in their match against MCC, an innings described by *Wisden* as a 'fine century'.

Blowers was a good stroke player but he never scored as fast as he talks. He gets twice as many words into a one-minute report as anyone else. And even when we have our discussions during the rain he speaks at machine-gun pace. He usually looks straight ahead of him and once he gets stuck into a subject, the words flow and it's difficult for anyone else to get a word in edgeways – and that's saying something in our box! On one occasion at Lord's it was pouring with rain at 2.30 p.m. and it was obvious that we had a long afternoon of talk ahead of us. We were all sitting in a row as Blowers got on to his favourite subject at the time – Kerry Packer. He went on and on at a tremendous pace looking straight out at the Nursery End, without so much as a glance at any of us.

After about four minutes we all got bored and left the box, leaving him to it. We then asked Peter Baxter to write something on a piece of paper and stick it in front of

Blower's face as he was in full spate. It read: 'KEEP GOING TILL 6.30 P.M.' I must say it temporarily stopped him in his tracks, as he looked round in panic and realized that he was alone in the box. He struggled for a few moments, and then we had mercy on him and filed back to our seats.

Blowers is delightful company, full of stories and anecdotes which are so full of details of time and place, that they do tend to go on a bit! Many of them are about his adventures on his trips abroad where at various times he appears to have been mugged, arrested, threatened by a cricket captain, and left standing stark naked in an hotel corridor. Wherever he goes he is followed or dated by a bevy of lovely girls and beauty queens. They chase him from continent to continent. What he has got, I am not sure. But the girls obviously like it. We could all learn from him. He is quite the best chatter-up in the business. He has become a cult with the Hillites at Sydney. Henry Blow-Fly they call him and there is a Henry Blow-Fly Fan Club. He goes across to the Hill to talk to them. As you will have gathered, talking plays a big part in his life, which is why he is such a good commentator and welcome member of the *T.M.S.* team. His most endearing habit is the way in which he apologizes for *everything*. No matter if it is not his fault; the box resounds with 'Sorry, sorry' when he is around. I firmly believe that if one accidentally shoved him off Beachy Head, he would be saying 'Sorry, sorry' as he fell towards the rocks below. Manners Makyth Man is the Winchester motto, not Eton's. But it applies to Blowers.

Bill Frindall

Bill's is the easiest nickname to explain. He has a black beard and is undoubtedly a wonder, so 'The Bearded Wonder' came quite naturally. He is the vital part of the commentary machine. All we commentators are easily expendable and replaceable. But it would be hard to replace the B.W. He came into broadcasting in 1966, following the sad death of the *T.M.S.* scorer Arthur Wrigley, just over a month after the end of the 1965 cricket season. He started scoring for the Temple Bar C.C. at the age of ten. After six years in which he began to learn about the history of cricket and its records, he then played club cricket. He is still an enthusiastic tearaway fast medium in-swing bowler, and a sound batsman who bats lower than he thinks he should. He does not have much spare time during a busy summer, but on any day when he is not in the box, he will be playing cricket somewhere. He is much in demand for Sunday charity matches and organizes his own tours abroad to places like Malta and Singapore. Woe betide me on the Monday of a Test Match if I forget to ask him over the air how he got on in his Sunday game.

He was in the RAF for six years and then was about to start life in the City as a life assurance inspector, when he heard the news of Arthur Wrigley's death. He had been keeping his own statistical records of first-class players for some time, and had studied the scoring methods of those three original BBC scorers (as they were called in those days), Arthur Wrigley, Roy Webber and Jack Price.

Bill has never been lacking in confidence and immediately decided to apply for the job as a replacement for Arthur. He came up to the BBC to see the cricket producer Michael Tuke-Hastings, and myself as cricket correspondent. We were struck by his confidence and obvious knowledge of cricket. But perhaps we were even more impressed by the lay-out and the neatness of the sample score-sheets which he brought with him. We had no doubt that he was our man and he was given a contract for the 1966 season, without our even seeing another applicant. There must have been many people who would have liked the job, though it meant giving up the whole of the summer to scoring in the Tests and county matches. But he was prepared to take the risk, and has been the regular Statistician on *T.M.S.* ever since. Note the new title which is well-earned. His scoring is vitally important and he has evolved a fairly complicated format based on the original Wrigley/Webber method. It tells the commentator all he wants to know – where each stroke has gone, the exact time anything has happened, the number of balls received off each bowler, the changes in the weather, details of all the extras, delays for the ball going out of shape, the statistics of the streaker and so on.

But in addition to all that, he can answer any question about individual cricketers, their records, results of past Test Matches, etc. He carries round with him a collection of books, many of which he has compiled himself. He may not be able to answer a question immediately, but he knows exactly where to look and in a few seconds all is revealed. While he is searching for the answer he has to keep the score, and sometimes to pull his leg we ask him how many balls there are left in the over, just as he is delving into some enormous tome. After catching him out once or twice he now regularly replies '*approximately*' two or three or whatever it may be.

But he does not just wait for us to ask him questions. He comes to each Test armed with up-to-date figures of any possible record that could be broken during that Test. He will either nudge the commentator to show that he is 'broody' and has some priceless piece of information or sometimes he will pass a note saying something like: '. . . If Bloggs hits another four he will have scored more boundaries in a Test hundred than any other Englishman.' When he does this while I am on the air I often bait him and say, 'I'm not too sure – my memory is not very good – but I think that if Bloggs hits another four he will have scored more boundaries . . . I'll just ask Bill Frindall to check up in his books.' It usually succeeds in getting a rise out of him, probably displayed by a big snort. He is an inveterate snorter whenever anything amuses him, which seems to be quite often. His microphone is only switched up when one of us asks him a deliberate question, so when he is trying to attract attention listeners can only hear his frantic whispers in the background.

He is usually first in the box every morning, bringing with him an amazing collection of books, pens, pencils, rubbers, calculator, a thermos, a cushion and three stop-watches. The cushion is vital because whereas we can get up and stretch our legs after our twenty-minute stints, he is stuck to his chair for the whole two-hour session. How he manages to concentrate for that length of time and do all the things he has to do against a fairly chaotic background of chatter, laughter and requests for information, I just don't know. He can do at least three things at once, including signing autograph books which are often thrust under his nose just as he is about to record the end of an over on his elaborate score-sheet. Those three stopwatches are important too. They hang on hooks in front of him, the one on the left showing the batting time of the batsman on the left of the main scoreboard; the centre one for the over-all time of the innings; and the right-hand one for the other batsman. At the start or close of play at any interval you can, if you listen carefully, hear three distinct clicks as he presses each watch as the first ball is bowled or the umpires take off the bails.

But in case you are beginning to feel sorry for the B.W., I must tell you that he arrives at each Test Match with a very attractive lady assistant, though not always the same one. She helps him carry his clobber, pours out his coffee, telephones his statistical copy to the papers and most important of all prepares and serves his lunch and tea. There's usually a small table with a white tablecloth, a bottle of wine, a starter, main course and sweet and cheese. He hurries from the box without waiting for the summary to finish, and arrives back just in time for the first ball after the interval.

The rest of us, unless asked to a tent or a box, usually have an 'airline' type of lunch kindly provided by the sponsors. But the B.W. prefers his 'waitress' service and I think that he deserves it.

He spends his life recording the feats and records of players. But he himself can boast one which is unique and unlikely to be broken. He has scored throughout one day of a Test at the Oval dressed as an Arab. He did it for a bet in 1977 when his hostess at a party offered him £62 – the proceeds of a collection among the guests – for his favourite charity if he could do it and get away with it. She got the idea because there was a genuine Arab at her party who offered to lend Bill his Arab costume and headdress, after thinking that with his black beard and swarthy appearance he really was an Arab. A few words of Arabic soon dissipated that idea!

Next morning the attendant at the Hobbs Gates at the

Oval thought that it was strange for an Arab to be driving a
car with a BBC sticker on it, but nevertheless signalled him
in. Bill immediately drove to his usual reserved parking
space by the back door of the Pavilion – specially reserved
because of all the books which he has to carry up to the
commentary box. A worried official ran up and shouted,
'Sorry, sir. You cannot park there. It's reserved for Bill
Frindall.' Bill wound down his window and said that he
couldn't care less for Mr Frindall: 'I have just bought the
Oval, and I shall park where I want to!' He then let the
embarrassed official into his secret, and made his way with
his briefcases through the already crowded longroom up to
the box.

When we all arrived later we noticed this Arab figure
sitting in Bill's usual corner. We were a bit suspicious but
didn't like to challenge him in case it was someone from the
BBC World Service who was to be attached to us for the
day. It wasn't until the first ball was about to be bowled
that we were confident that it must be the Bearded Wonder,
and we got him to tell the listeners the story. I am glad to
say that he stayed in his Arab dress all day and so won his
bet. He told us, by the way, that his white robes were called
Dish Dash and had once belonged to King Hussein, who
had given them away to a friend. 'I don't blame him!' said
Fred Trueman.

Tony Lewis

The most recent addition to the *T.M.S.* team is Tony
Lewis, known to us all as ARL, to the annoyance of his
wife. I'm afraid that I am to blame once again. I was coming
to the end of my commentary stint and glanced at the rota
for the commentators, pinned up in front of me. Peter
Baxter puts just our initials, and there, sure enough, I saw
that the next man in to follow me was A.R.L., and – I'm
sorry, Mrs Lewis – I simply said, 'And now after a few
words from Trevor Bailey, ARL will take over the commentary.' And so it has stuck. He started with us in 1979
and brought an air of great distinction to the box. Here we
had an ex-Captain of England, and of Cambridge. A double

blue for cricket and rugby and to his credit the fine feat of making ninety-five as a Freshman in the Varsity match at Lord's, and then two years later in 1962 making 103 not out when captain. Added to all this were a hundred for England and the winning of the County Championship by Glamorgan when he was captain in 1969.

So we were very proud of our new recruit, who was no stranger to television or radio. In Wales he had hosted both an Arts and weekly sports programme on TV, while on Radio 4 his *Sport on 4* on Saturday morning had become a high-class sports magazine presented in a friendly and highly personalized style. Later he was to be one of the presenters of the TV show *Saturday Night at the Mill*. In fact it was during one of these programmes which always went out 'live' that the string of his violin went flat due to the heat of the studio lights, when he was slap in the middle of the Handel Violin Sonata. Yes, believe it or not, he is also a skilled musician and was a member of the Glamorgan Youth Orchestra. Indeed on one occasion he had to choose between playing for the Welsh National Youth Orchestra, or for Glamorgan *v* Leicestershire, and he chose the latter.

There was never any doubt in anyone's mind that he would be a success at commentating. Not just because of his cricketing knowledge and experience. But to a man who could cope in a live television interview – as he did one Saturday night at the Mill – with Oliver Reed, who proceeded to take off his trousers in the middle of the interview – being a mere commentator would be a 'piece of cake'. (And he would get plenty of that in the box.)

He started off doing the summaries and reports and gradually eased into the commentary seat. In fact he did not find it too easy at first, partly because he had been doing some television commentary. He found it difficult to keep a flow of talk going, and there were one or two long pauses, which of course would be completely acceptable on television. He had one other difficulty. He got so absorbed in the cricket – as you would expect from an ex-England captain – that he often forgot to give the score and was inclined to ignore Bill Frindall's feed of records then being or about to be broken. I still think he finds these the most difficult things about commentary. He has a soft, lilting Welsh voice with a friendly chuckle, and as if he hadn't got enough already, he is by far and away the best-looking commentator on either radio or television – not that there is too much competition!

His other considerable skill is his writing, and as the *Sunday Telegraph* cricket correspondent he puts forward his point of view and opinions in an entertaining and forthright manner. This job also enables him to tour abroad in the winter and he has broadcast for the BBC from Pakistan, the West Indies, India and Australia. There seems to be no limit to his activities, and as I write he is presenting the sports news on BBC 2 *Newsnight*.

Christopher Martin-Jenkins

Jenkers is the man of many voices, and his mimicry and impersonations come up to the highest professional standard. Indeed at one Lord's Taverners' Lunch he spoke first and produced many of his impersonations, not just of sportsmen and television personalities, but also of politicians. He brought the house down and made things very difficult for the star impersonator who had to speak after him. He can do almost anyone, even me! But he is shy about doing it in front of me, though I did once catch him taking off my rather ridiculous hyena-like laugh.

I first met him when he was still a schoolboy at Marlborough where he was two years in the first eleven. He was captain in his second year but alas Marlborough were beaten at Lord's by Rugby, though Jenkers himself made 99, thus missing by one the chance to join his fellow commentators Blofeld and Lewis as a century-maker at Lord's. That was in 1963, the year in which I became the BBC's first cricket correspondent. I received a letter from him during the summer term asking for my advice on how to become a cricket commentator (I still get letters asking the same question). I asked him to come up to the BBC to meet me and, so he reminds me, I gave him lunch in the BBC Club in the old Langham Hotel. I did my best to encourage him, and told him – as I tell everyone – to get a tape-recorder and go out and describe anything and everything. Obviously a cricket match would be ideal. But the object is to say to oneself: 'I will now talk non-stop for fifteen minutes, and imagine that I am trying to describe what I am seeing to a blind man' (one who has *gone* blind, not been *born* blind, which makes a visual explanation more or less impossible).

He went up to Cambridge where, although he failed to get a cricket blue, he and his brother became famous for their impersonations, rather in the style of Tony Fayne and David Evans. He did, however, play for Surrey's second eleven but with his goal still the same after five years. He wanted above everything else to be a cricket commentator. There are hundreds of young boys who have the same dream but, since there are only about ten cricket commentators who can achieve Test Match status at one time, it is a more-or-less impossible dream. You must have luck, which is just what Jenkers had. In 1968 Jim Swanton appointed him Assistant Editor of the *Cricketer* and for two years he was able to live cricket, absorbing the atmosphere, getting to know all the players and administrators, and learning how to report and write about cricket. It was an invaluable schooling and in 1970 he had no difficulty in getting a job in the BBC Radio Sports Department of O.B.s, where he continued to learn about reporting and commentating on cricket, but now as a broadcaster, and not as a writer. In 1972 I retired as a member of the BBC staff and so had to relinquish the job of Cricket Correspondent. After a year's gap, Jenkers was appointed in my place and did the job for seven years, before going freelance in 1980, and becoming Editor of the *Cricketer*.

Those seven years were for him in some ways immensely satisfying, but in another way extremely frustrating. He went on all the tours with MCC and broadcast commentary back to this country. In addition there came more and more demands from the News on Radio 4 and the many sports bulletins on Radio 2 for one-minute reports on the Tests and other games. Unfortunately he became so good at doing them that when he was back here in the summer he found he was being given all the reports to do, and very little commentary.

But gradually people have come to realize what a good commentator he is, as well as a reporter, and he is now a fully-fledged member of the commentary team. In addition he has done one or two Tests for television and has taken over John Arlott's place on the BBC 2 TV coverage of the Sunday John Player League matches. He is clear and articulate with a very young voice in contrast to the more mature voices of some of his colleagues.

This *should* be an advantage, but strangely in cricket – as opposed to the faster moving games like soccer and rugby – listeners tend to be a bit suspicious of youth. 'What does *he* know about it? He sounds too young to know. . . .' But Jenkers overcomes this because of his accurate and perceptive description of the play, and his immense background knowledge of the administrative set-up, the laws and regulations, and details of the players themselves. As Editor of the *Cricketer* he is at the hub of affairs and is often 'in the know', whereas someone like myself who no longer does cricket reports and news interviews, is not.

He can also boast the slimmest figure in the commentary box. He is tall, lean and willowy with a jaunty walk and often looks as if he might be blown over by a strong wind! He is invaluable in our many discussions because he has strong views which he is happy to defend and argue about. As part owner of a horse called Twickenham, he is sometimes able to help us to beat the bookies. He is really a priceless asset to the BBC, should the latter ever wish to economize drastically. He could, on his own, carry out a day's commentary so that the listeners would think that we were all in the box taking our turn every twenty minutes. He can imitate the summarizers as well. I really think he could get away with it, though it might be a bit exhausting.

The more I write about my colleagues the more I realize that I am on my own as a gaffe-maker. None of them seems to make the mistakes or *double entendres* that I do. I did however catch Jenkers once during the summer of 1982. We had been talking about a man in the crowd with a bald head. I can't remember the reason. Anyhow, Jenkers tried to refer to him on one occasion and instead of calling him, as he intended, 'Our bald-headed friend,' he said, 'Our bald-freddied hen'! Still, he has many years ahead of him and he will probably do better than that!

In spite of his slender frame he has great energy and an enormous capacity for work. On all his tours, in spite of commentating all day and doing interviews and reports at all hours of the day, he used to write a book on the tour in question, which meant that while others were relaxing after a well-earned dinner, he would be upstairs tapping away at his typewriter behind closed doors. His editorials in the *Cricketer* are full of sound sense and judgement and he is a firm advocate of the right way in which cricket should be played.

If he has a failing it could be that he tends to give Peter Baxter a heart attack whenever he is due to take over commentary. He is seldom waiting in the box but hurriedly appears just as the other commentator has said, 'Over now to Christopher Martin –.' Oh, and one other thing I nearly forgot. Anyone who is in the box when he is commentating is advised to put cotton wool in their ears, against the moment when a batsman is out or there is some dramatic action on the field. On these occasions Jenkers' high-pitched shout is the envy of every drill sergeant at the Guards Training Depot at Caterham!

Don Mosey

My tendency to give people nicknames is a fairly harmless habit which I hope gives more amusement than annoyance. Even when I was in the Grenadier Guards during the war our mess sergeant became 'Uncle Tom', my technical clerks were 'Honest Joe' and 'Burglar Bill' – and so on. And what's more the regular peacetime Grenadier officers so far forgot their tradition of strict discipline that they too used the nicknames. The success of a nickname depends on whether it sticks. Three of my own favourites were 'Melon' (for the Australian Test Cricketer D. J. Colley), 'The Hatchet' (for an officer friend called Berry) and 'Nymph' (for umpire David Constant).

This brings me to The Alderman – the name with which I saddled Don Mosey some years ago. People often ask us how it came about, whilst agreeing that the title suits him well. It started when a broadcast of the Radio 2 quiz-game *Treble Chance* was going out from the Lancaster Town Hall. Don was organizing the broadcast on behalf of BBC North Region, and he seemed to me to fit in well with all the dignified trappings of the Mayor's Parlour and Council Chamber. So from that moment I elected him The Alderman, which he has gracefully accepted ever since.

He is another of our *T.M.S.* team who by his character and background brings contrast to our commentaries. He lives in Morecambe and his office is in Manchester. Both in Lancashire. But forget that – he is a Yorkshireman born in Keighley, who played his first League Cricket match at the age of eleven. So, incidentally, did Brian Close and they both made eleven not out on their debut. He then combined playing rugby and cricket with reporting sport for the press and can boast one performance which must rival anyone else's best in the commentary box. In one game he made 100 in forty-five minutes and took 7 for 28 including a hat trick. He was an opening bat and fast bowler and after the war, when he served in India, he played League Cricket and in benefit matches whenever his journalistic duties allowed. After reporting for the *Daily Express* and then writing on county cricket for the *Daily Mail*, he came to the BBC in Manchester, combining producing with broadcasting. In addition to cricket, he commentates on rugby and golf. He sometimes has the pleasure of describing the play of his son Ian, now one of the country's top golf professionals. Don had hoped that Ian would play cricket for Yorkshire, and to make sure sent his wife Jo back to Yorkshire from Nottingham *three months* before the birth!

Don has all the characteristics of a true Yorkshireman. This means that he is blunt, honest, obstinate and says exactly what he thinks. He tries to be a perfectionist in all he does, setting himself a very high standard. As a result he finds it difficult to tolerate inefficiency in others, so that when he speaks his mind he is bound to offend some people. He sees most things in black or white, and eschews compromise, determined to defend his principles whatever the cost. He is the complete traditionalist – Queen and Country, strict standards of behaviour and discipline, and, needless to say, orthodox three-day cricket as opposed to the limited-over competitions.

There was a perfect example of his innate traditionalism during the summer of 1982. He is an ardent devotee of the D'Oyly Carte Gilbert and Sullivan operas. With his friend Phil Sharpe at the piano he can sing his way through all the songs. When the American version of *Pirates of Penzance* opened at Drury Lane I saw it and thought it was a wonderful production – lively, fast-moving, with magnificent choreography and a brassy band as opposed to the rather thin orchestrations of D'Oyly Carte. It was really more of a pantomime than an opera. I implored him to go and see it if only to compare it with the traditional presentation. But he was adamant, and refused to go. It was sacrilege to interfere with something which had been such a success for so many years.

I have devoted quite a bit of space to trying to portray Don's character, because it is all reflected in his commentary. His style is laconic and conversational with a very precise choice of words. He does not flow non-stop and get too excited, as some of us do. He reports calmly what he sees, and if he approves or disapproves he will say so. Once again out comes the Yorkshire honesty. If he is bored he will admit it, and will not try to build up something which doesn't exist. He has a deep knowledge of cricket based partly on his own playing experience, but even more on his close association and friendship with many of the first-class players – especially with the Yorkshire players like Brian Close, Freddie Trueman and Ray Illingworth. A rare combination of skills and tactical sense.

He has toured all the Test-playing countries with one important exception – Australia, and that is probably the biggest disappointment of his life. He had gradually built up to what was to be the pinnacle of his broadcasting career. On his other tours his reports were typically honest about the hotels, the food, the broadcasting conditions and the travel. His weekly newsletter was a model description of places visited and the goings-on of the England team. But inevitably some of his criticisms – no matter how true –

offended some people. As, for instance, from India during the England tour of 1981/82 when he admittedly was not too complimentary about some of the conditions. But ironically he had been stationed in India as a soldier, and loves the country. This was evident in many of his reports but it was the words of criticism that stuck in people's minds.

Anyhow, the BBC did not send him to Australia, and this was a body blow to him. Underneath the tough Yorkshire crust is an extremely sensitive and emotional man and I only hope that he will not be discouraged from broadcasting cricket in the future. After all, it has been the happiest work of his life.

The reason for the BBC's decision was largely because of a change of policy in broadcasting from Australia. Before 1982 the BBC had sent out its own commentator to join the ABC commentary team, whose output was then relayed back to England. But due to complicated contractual difficulties, ABC were now to broadcast on their own, and the BBC to set up their own broadcasting unit, as they had done both in India and Pakistan. This meant that, unlike in the past, a producer – Peter Baxter – had to go out to arrange and produce all the many transmissions back to England, and no commentator was to be sent out especially from England. The broadcasting team would be made up of commentators already in Australia as correspondents for newspapers and magazines, or for other reasons, thus saving air fares. Henry Blofeld was there for all the Tests since he writes for a number of papers. Tony Lewis for the *Sunday Telegraph* and Chris Martin-Jenkins for the *Cricketer* were also there for some of the Tests. And I too was one of the lucky ones, having determined to go to Sydney to visit my son and combine it with the fifth Test Match.

All small comfort I'm afraid for The Alderman. The England team will have missed his skill at Scrabble, and the Australian public will not have seen him in his shorts – a sight I myself have not had the privilege to see.

The Alderman is a terrible giggler, and the slightest thing seems to set him off. This tempts one to play tricks on him as we did once when he was in the commentary seat and had just received a card from Peter Baxter instructing him to 'WELCOME WORLD SERVICE'. This he did and went on with his commentary. A few minutes later we put another card in front of him. 'WELCOME LISTENERS IN THE VIRGIN ISLANDS, AND EXPLAIN THAT THEIR POSITION IS SOME CONSIDERABLE DISTANCE FROM THE ISLE OF MAN.' This of course had the desired effect.

Edgbaston is an unlucky ground for the Alderman. Whenever we are broadcasting from there Cyril Goodway, the chairman, kindly comes along and stands in front of our box to take orders for pre-lunch drinks. He makes various signs through the glass which we all understand, and he then notes down our requirements. On the first occasion Don broadcast with us at Edgbaston he knew nothing of this very civilized custom. He was on the air when Cyril appeared as usual at about 12.30. 'Oh,' said The Alderman. 'I can't see what's going on. Some stupid idiot is making tic tac signs at me through the window. He must be crackers.' We hurriedly wrote an explanation on a piece of paper but it was a poor return to Cyril for all his kindness over the years!

I shall go on looking forward to the Word Game Championships Don and I play (see page 163). I am always amazed that, in spite of all his knowledge of the English language, I am usually in the lead at the end of the season. And whatever may happen in the future, I hope he will always continue to send me those rude seaside postcards from Morecambe.

Freddie Trueman

Life in the commentary box has never been the same since Freddie joined Trevor Bailey as our other regular expert summarizer. He is outsize in everything – his figure, his personality, his pipe, his stories and his down-to-earth no-nonsense comments on what he sees out in the middle. Like another great Yorkshireman, Sir Harold Wilson, Fred has an astonishing memory. His knowledge of cricket, its records and its players is phenomenal. He and I do our best to stump each other with quiz questions. I am easy meat but I can very rarely catch him out. He played his cricket with such astute tacticians and technicians as Hutton, Illingworth and Close and he has obviously stored everything he saw or heard in his 'little grey cells'. He might in fact have made a great captain, and can at least be proud of his achievement in 1968. In the absence of Brian Close he captained Yorkshire against the Australians at Sheffield and Yorkshire beat them for the first time since 1902 by an innings and sixty-nine runs.

As I have said, he is down-to-earth in everything he says, and I must say is extremely fair. He will praise or criticize as the occasion warrants and express himself strongly in either case. He is undoubtedly a bit puzzled by some of the modern cricket tactics and has a favourite phrase: 'I don't know what's going off out there.' And I must admit that I often agree with him! He is at his most critical about the modern fast bowlers, particularly as regards their actions and their fitness. Inevitably it may seem to some listeners that he is looking at the past through rose-coloured spectacles. But if anyone is honest – as of course every Yorkshireman is – he or she must agree that the standard of play in first-class cricket *has* dropped, except for fielding, throwing, and running between the wickets.

Fred, as you can imagine, is never lost for words or the apt phrase and his sense of humour comes through in all he says. He is one of the finest raconteurs in the country and can entertain an audience with non-stop stories or one-liners for well over an hour. Nor are they all Rabelaisian. Mention any subject and he probably has a story about it, and can always cap anyone else's stories. His best two-liner in the commentary box was once when it was raining at the Oval. 'What's the fastest thing on two wheels in London?' he asked us. None of us knew. 'An Arab riding a bicycle through Golders Green!'

He also enjoys the simple jokes that are often sent in to us:

B.J.:   If you were stark naked out in a snowstorm, what animal would you like to be, Fred?

F.S.T.:   I dunno, Johnners, let's have it.

> B.J.: A little otter.

or

> B.J.: Who was the ice-cream man in the Bible?
> F.S.T.: All right. I'll buy it.
> B.J. Walls of Jericho.

After I had told this joke a listener wrote in to me and asked, 'What about Lyons of Judah?'

I normally call Fred 'Sir Frederick' and this led to an amusing incident. I had written a book and asked my publisher to send a copy to all the members of *T.M.S.* I wrote something in each book and in Fred's wrote something like:

> To Sir Frederick, with happy memories of days in the commentary box.

I thought no more about it until Peter Baxter told me what followed. One morning Fred's postman ran up to his front door, shouting, 'You've got it, at last, Fred,' and when Fred opened the door, there was a parcel addressed to *Sir* Frederick Trueman. The secretary at my publishers had read what I had written, and addressed the book parcel accordingly. What Fred said then would not have been entirely acceptable in the commentary box! But in his politer moments he did tell Peter that 'that Johnners is a right one.'

He has undoubtedly added great weight to our commentary team. He can speak with the confidence of a man who took 307 Test wickets. He brings a strong northern flavour to contrast with the more southerly tones and attitudes of all of us in the box, except for Don Mosey. I know that Fred loves every minute of his time with us. We enjoy having him too and value all his cricketing knowledge and experience, although we are never *quite* sure what he's coming out with next. Of one thing, though, we can be sure. He will always be creating a smoke-screen with his vast pipe or Lew Grade cigars. The resulting smell is pretty pungent, so we have called Fred's cigars 'Adam and Eve' – every time he's Adam, we Eve! But it's a small price to pay, and he wouldn't be Fred without them.

Part Four Mixed Bag

The One Who Got Away

Among my commentators, I am including someone who, although he did do a little commentary, opted finally for administration. Had he stuck to commentating he could, I think, have been one of the best ever. He is certainly one of the most versatile and gifted of performers. He is the Welsh Rugby Union International, Cliff Morgan – the most-capped fly-half for Wales with twenty-nine caps and a member of that victorious British Lions side in South Africa in 1955 when they won a sensational match 23–22 at Johannesburg. He is still spoken of with awe in Wales and for nine years held the rugby crowds spellbound with his brilliant running, jinking and passing.

When he left Tonyrefail Grammar School in South Wales his sports master said of him, 'Not much good in class – his biggest asset is his buttocks.' He joined the BBC in 1958 and has done almost everything there is to do – quiz master, disc jockey, presenter of *All Your Own*, *Songs of Praise* and *These You Have Loved*. He was Editor of *Sportsview* and *Grandstand* and Producer of *This Week* for ITV. After a spell of freelance writing and broadcasting he became first Editor of Radio Sport, then Head of Radio Outside Broadcasts from 1974 to 1975. But Television was quick to capture him and since 1975 he has been Head of BBC Television O.B.s. This means that except for the occasional job of introducing a programme on radio, his performing activities have been restricted to after-dinner speaking at which he is outstanding, one of the best in the country.

Cliff has all the attributes of the perfect commentator – a distinctive Welsh voice with a chuckle in it; he is enthusiastic, witty and highly emotional and weeps as easily as he laughs. He is a good raconteur and his lively personality is infectious. Not surprisingly he enjoys a party and plays the piano and sings with the best of them, especially Welsh hymns. His hobby is music, about which he is very knowledgeable. Unfortunately, except for a spell at rugby he has done little commentary and one can only guess what heights he might have reached. But he has always enjoyed his various top administrative jobs, as indeed he enjoys everything. He has the right assessment of the commentator's job: 'Our duty,' he once said, 'is not to the ego, but to the audience.' Very salutary advice. I only wish that I could cross my heart and say that I have always followed it.

Cliff is an amazing character. He is here, there and everywhere, making long excursions into deepest Wales for concerts, dinners or gatherings, and often returning the same night to be at his desk at Kensington House first thing next morning. Remarkable really. Because in 1972 while in Germany he suffered a severe stroke and was out of things for eleven months. But he has this great energy and unflagging spirit and just goes on and on. A sad loss to commentary but a big asset to the organization and running of sport on BBC Television.

The Last Word

The BBC has always reserved the right to choose their own commentators and not to be influenced by any outside body. There have been several instances of sporting officials complaining about what a commentator has said and hinting that it might be better if he were dropped. But the BBC has always stood firm, with one exception: an occasion when a commentator selected by the BBC to cover a match was banned from entering the ground where it was taking place. This occurred in 1951 when the Welsh rugby commentator G. V. (Geevers) Wynne-Jones was refused entry to Cardiff Arms Park for the Wales *v* Ireland match. Geevers had written a book in which he claimed that certain Welsh clubs were paying their players by surreptitious means. The Welsh Rugby Union asked him to reveal the names of the clubs, but Geevers somewhat naturally refused. Hence their ban and the BBC were forced to find another commentator.

For What It's Worth . . .

For Test Matches both BBC Television and Radio give cricket a magnificent coverage. But otherwise it takes very much of a back seat. Soccer – in spite of its falling standards and gates, and the hooliganism, reigns supreme. It's like the back pages of the tabloids. The Sports Editors give soccer all the space and headlines.

Inevitably in the BBC you get producers and presenters who just don't understand cricket, except possibly the limited-over game. Nowadays everyone seems to want immediate action and results. When Cricket Correspondent I had to fight hard to get cricket any coverage on programmes like *Sportsview* on BBC Television. This was produced by Paul Fox who had always been suspicious of cricket's entertainment value. He just did not understand it. I remember once when we were televising a county match and he was producing *Grandstand*. We had been broadcasting for almost a quarter of an hour, when I heard him say into my headphones: 'Right-ho Johnners. We'll leave you at the end of this over. Let me know when the next wicket is going to fall and we'll come back to you for it!'

Chestnut Corner

As most listeners to *Test Match Special* must already know

only too well, we do produce some pretty terrible jokes during pauses in play. Some are sent in by listeners, others are the result of my past visits to the music halls, when they existed. Most of the jokes are vintage and corny in the extreme, but at least the majority are clean! They also need a straight man, and my colleagues – especially Trevor and Fred – usually sportingly oblige. You will by now have come across some of the best and worst, but here are several more which we have perpetrated during the last few years:

– What's the difference between a stoat and a weasel?
– One's stoately different, the other is weasily distinguished.

* * *

– If a fly is flying from China to England, and a flea flying from England to China, what is the time in China when they meet half-way?
– Fly past Flea (3.05 p.m.).

* * *

– What did the two fleas say as they flew off Robinson Crusoe?
– See you on Friday.

* * *

– The Invisible Man is outside.
– Tell him I can't see him today.

* * *

– I call my dog Trueman because he has four short legs and his balls swing both ways.

* * *

– My wife doesn't like soft sugar.
– What do you do about it?
– Make her lump it!

* * *

– On my way to the ground I saw forty men under one umbrella and not one of them got wet.
– It must have been a very large umbrella.
– No, it wasn't raining.

* * *

– What would you like to drink?
– I'll have a mother-in-law, please.
– What's that?
– Stout and bitter.

* * *

– My parents are in the iron and steel business. My mother irons, my father steals.

* * *

– What's your brother doing these days?
– Nothing.
– But I thought he got that job as Producer of *Test Match Special*?
– Yes. He got the job.

* * *

And there I think I had better stop!

For Whom the Bell Tolls

From our commentary box at Lord's we can always hear the bell of St John's Church ringing for Evensong, just before close of play. I usually make a comment about it, as it's my parish church where all my five children have been christened and my daughter married. Some years ago our Rector was called Noel Perry-Gore and when I met him the other day he told me of how he had won a bet with his children. They were listening to me commentating from Lord's one lunchtime, whether on television or radio I am not sure. He said to his children: 'I bet you I can make Brian Johnston mention St John's Church during his commentary.'

Of course they thought he was joking, so took him on. With that, he ran out of the rectory, went into the church, and rang the bell lustily. After about a minute's ringing, he went back to his children. They were in a state of great excitement: 'You've won, Daddy,' they said. 'Just now

Brian Johnston said, "That's the bell of St John's Church, by the roundabout at the Nursery End. I wonder what on earth it's ringing for at this time of day. The Rector must have heard some good news from somewhere." '

'It's All Right Leaving Here'

If ever there is a technical hitch and an outside broadcast goes off the air, more often than not we hear the engineer at the broadcasting point say the above. In other words, the fault is not at our end, but somewhere in the Post Office lines, the switching centre or the control room back at base. I have written mostly about the commentators in this book – the front men. But I can never stress enough that without the backroom boys our efforts are useless. They have the tough job of setting everything up the day before, and before a Test Match this can be a long and difficult job with some-times as many as ten microphones including those for the commentators, sound effects, World Service, Radio 4 and Radio 2 reporters. Then follows five days of intense con-centration, listening to every word, and watching the needle to make sure that the volume is at the right level, even when a commentator raises his voice to describe some exciting event out in the middle. And at the end of the match when we can all relax or rush off home, they have the unenviable task of dismantling all the gear.

Thankfully, as I have said earlier, one of the great joys of working in Outside Broadcasts is the marvellous rela-tionship which has always existed between commentators and engineers. Both realize it is a fifty-fifty team effort and there has also always been pride in the output of the depart-ment and the need to try to maintain the highest possible standard.

I have been lucky all my time at the BBC to have enjoyed

this friendship with the engineers with whom I have worked. Not just at the cricket, but also on my 'Let's Go Somewhere' feature for *In Town Tonight*, on Royal Occasions and of course on *Down Your Way*, which, although it has to be recorded, is still regarded as an O.B. Together we have shared successes and one or two disasters but never have there been any temperamental scenes. We have also shared, at the cricket, many of the cakes, sweets and other delicacies which listeners so kindly send us. At the end of every day I always try to remember to pop my head into their control box to say 'thank you', and I would like to say it again now to *all* my engineering friends with whom I have worked over the thirty-seven years.

Absent Friends

I am sure that after reading this book some of you will say, 'Oh, he hasn't mentioned so-and-so.' And you will be quite right. I have only written about other commentators with whom I have had the pleasure of working in O.B.s. Ever since I left the BBC in 1972 there has been a steady influx of new commentators, especially in the worlds of soccer, rugby and athletics. I have met and worked with many of them in various sports programmes but not on an outside broadcast, as I have really only been concerned with cricket and the Boat Race, as far as sports commentary is concerned.

I greatly admire all their slick expertise and am always happy to read if one of them follows my bad example and makes a gaffe. I particularly enjoy listening to Alan Parry, whose descriptions of soccer and athletics tell me all I want to know. Alas, I did not hear him say it but he is reputed to have made the following comment after a goal had been scored: 'And that goal gives him his eleventh goal of the season so far – *exactly* double what he scored last year.' He also once said, 'With the last *kick* of the game Bobby McDonald scored a *header*'!

Goals seem to have a funny effect on commentators. One of them on B B C T V once said after a particularly dramatic goal in the last minute of a match: '. . . and I felt a lump in my throat as the ball went in'!

Racing commentators make surprisingly few gaffes, which is remarkable considering the speed at which they have to talk and the number of names which they have to mention. I know that I should get into a lot of trouble, just as John Oaksey, that genial racing front man for I T V, once did. There were very few runners in a race at York and John was having difficulty finding any more to say about the horses as they paraded round the paddock. Major Petch, the Clerk of the Course, had recently had built a raised concrete bank round the paddock to enable more people to see the horses. John began to talk about this innovation and as a cue to get the cameras on to it, said, 'So let's look at Major Petch's erection.' Then, realizing what he had said, he went on, 'Perhaps I should call it Major Petch's stand'!

Anyhow, as usual I am digressing. I would like to wish all these commentators – as well as those whom I have mentioned – as much happiness, fun, enjoyment and job satisfaction as I have had during my broadcasting life. Commentators are a unique band. There are very few of us, and in spite of the travel, long hours, the stresses and the working conditions – often too cramped, too hot or too cold – we should all be extremely grateful for having such a wonderful job. People *do* sometimes complain, forgetting how lucky they are and that there are so many millions of people far worse off than themselves. Perhaps this story will remind them.

There was a young parachutist about to make his first jump from an aeroplane, and he was naturally very nervous and scared. His instructor tried to calm him down and told him that there was nothing to worry about.

'Just remember,' he said, 'when I give you a push count five and then pull the top ring on your parachute. *If*, by any chance, nothing happens, don't panic. Just count another five, and then pull the bottom ring. This will open your reserve parachute, and you will sail gracefully down to earth. Nothing to worry about at all.'

The learner was still shivering with fright but when they were at the right height and place, the instructor told him, 'Right, I am going to push you out now. Don't forget. Count five – top ring – count another five – bottom ring. And whatever you do, don't panic. Off you go. Good luck.'

With that, he pushed the learner out of the plane. The young man remembered what he had been told. He counted five, pulled the top ring and waited for something to happen. Nothing did. So again he remembered what he had been told. He counted another five and confidently pulled the bottom ring. But again – this time to his horror – nothing happened. His pace increased and he was dropping at an alarming rate down to earth, when he suddenly spotted someone coming *up* towards him. It was a man in a peak cap and overalls, carrying a large spanner.

The parachutist – now in a complete state of panic – shouted at this man as he shot upwards towards him:

'Help! Help! Do you know anything about parachutes?'

'No, I'm afraid I don't,' replied the man in the peak cap as he shot past him. 'And what's more, I obviously know bugger all about gas boilers!'

I Know That Voice

All commentators have always used their Christian names in their billings, with a few exceptions: before the war it was always 'R. C. Lyle' and, to start with, 'Captain H. B. T. Wakelam', though this soon became 'Teddy'. The most obvious post-war exception was E. W. Swanton, known of course to everyone who worked with him as 'Jim'. But in the *Radio*

Times and when the announcer cued over it was always 'E.W.' which lent a certain air of mystery and dignity.

It's difficult to believe but in 1937 there was some talk at the BBC of not letting listeners know the identity of commentators. Not surprisingly, it came to nothing, though it's worth remembering that until the war all announcers and newsreaders were unnamed. During the war it was felt that for the sake of security it was better for the announcer to identify himself, so that the public could match the voice with a name. But in 1937 there was a typical reaction to the suggestion of anonymity in a letter of protest in the *Morning Post* which was headed: 'Hands off our friends the commentators'.

However, there were at least two who preserved their anonymity. The first was an Irish Rugby Football commentator, obviously not very experienced, who said, 'Now one of the forwards has got the ball – I can't say who he is – wait while I look at the programme – No. 8 – oh, well, it doesn't matter anyway, the other side has just scored a try'!

The other unknown achieved momentary fame during the Coronation celebrations in 1937. The BBC had set up a position at Canada Gate – just opposite Buckingham Palace. For several days and nights the News would cue over for a report on the scenes outside the Palace. There was a rota of commentators and news reporters who took it in turns to man the position which was in the charge of a BBC staff man called Neil Hutchinson.

One night just before the evening news bulletin a young man and his girlfriend in the crowd climbed up to the position, and unexpectedly found the door to the commentary box open. So they went inside and got down to a bit of a cuddle. They were soon interrupted by the arrival of a BBC engineer. On seeing the young man, he assumed it was Neil Hutchinson, whom he had never met. As there was no reporter there, the engineer said to the man he thought was Hutchinson, 'Are you going to do the insert into the news?' The young man was so staggered that he stammered out 'Yes'. The engineer gave him a microphone and told him to go ahead when the red light went on, and when it went off it would mean that the News had faded him out. He then told News all was ready and they said they would come over straight away and wanted a descriptive piece of about two minutes.

The young man was obviously terrified but the engineer merely thought he was a bit nervous. Remarkably, when the red light came on, the young man started to talk – admittedly in rather a halting manner. But somehow he managed to describe what he could see happening in front of the Palace and was still talking when they faded him out. News seemed perfectly satisfied and so was the engineer.

Naturally enough the young man boasted to friends of what he had done and somehow the *Daily Express* got hold of the story of this 'unknown broadcaster'. As a result the young man was invited to appear in *In Town Tonight* but sadly the high-ups in the BBC would not allow it.

The Definitive and Complete List of My Gaffes

At Headingley Test, 1961, as TV camera panned in to show Neil Harvey fielding at leg-slip: 'There's Neil Harvey, standing at leg-slip with his legs wide apart, waiting for a tickle.'

At Hove, Sussex *v* Hampshire, on radio, trying to describe Henry Horton's funny stance in which he crouches and sticks his bottom out: 'Henry Horton's got a funny sort of stance. It looks as if he's shitting on a sooting stick.'

At Southampton at close of play when handing over to Rex Alston at Edgbaston: 'It's close of play here but they go on till seven o'clock at Edgbaston. So over now for some more balls from Rex Alston.'

At Leicester on radio during a county match: 'As you come over, Ray Illingworth has just relieved himself at the Pavilion End.'

At Northampton in a match *v* Worcestershire, on radio: '. . . a very disappointing crowd. In fact I would say that there are more cars here than people.' (Who drove the cars in?!)

At Lord's during the Test in 1969, England *v* New Zealand. Alan Ward is playing in his first Test and bowling very fast from the Pavilion End. Off the *fifth* ball of one of his overs he hits Glenn Turner a terrible blow in the box. Glenn collapses in the crease, bat flying in one direction, his batting gloves in another. The TV camera pans in and shows him writhing in the crease. B.J. waffles away pretending Turner's been hit anywhere except where he has – as it's rude! At last, after a few minutes, Glenn Turner gets shakily to his feet, someone hands him his bat, someone else his gloves. B.J.: 'It looks as if he is going to try to continue, although he still looks very shaken and pale. Very plucky of him. Yes, he's definitely going to have a try: one ball left'!

At Old Trafford the Saturday of the Test between England and India. It's pouring with rain, and is cold and miserable. There are some Indian supporters huddled together looking miserable in the crowd. Radio 3 announcer cues over to B.J. at 11.25 a.m.: 'Any chance of a start, Brian?' B.J.: 'No, it's pelting with rain, and cold and miserable. No chance of any play at the moment. There's a dirty black crowd (cloud) here!'

At Worcester, Worcestershire *v* Hampshire, B.J.: 'Welcome to Worcester where you've just missed seeing Barry Richards hit one of Basil d'Oliveira's balls clean out of the ground.' (Loud laughter at the back of the commentary box.)

At Scarborough Festival, Peter Pollock has come over

from South Africa to play for Rest of World, and is on his honeymoon. As he runs up to bowl, he slips and turns his ankle over, and lies in obvious pain on the grass. B.J., on TV: 'Bad luck on Peter. He's obviously in great pain and has probably sprained his ankle. It's especially bad luck as he is here on his honeymoon with his pretty young wife. Still, he'll probably be all right tomorrow, if he sticks it up tonight.' (Collapse of Denis Compton in the commentary box.)

A lady wrote to me after a Test at the Oval between England and the West Indies. She said how much she enjoyed my commentaries but that I must be more careful, as there were always a lot of young people listening. She asked if I realized what I had said when Michael Holding was bowling to Peter Willey. Evidently at the start of an over I had said: 'The bowler's Holding the batsman's Willey.'

When commentating for radio outside St Paul's Cathedral for the wedding of Prince Charles and Lady Diana I found myself saying: 'I can see the bride's procession coming up Ludgate Hill. When she arrives below me here at St Paul's she will walk with her father up the steps into the pavilion – er – I mean Cathedral.'

Postscript: Last Over

There is an old *Punch* joke in which, on a beautiful April morning, a hearty chap greets a passing friend with the words, 'Spring in the air!' To which his rather pompous friend replies, 'I have no inclination to do so!'

Well, as I write this, spring is in the air: the blossom is out and a new cricket season is just about to start. Already I have been up the road to Lord's, and have seen the schoolboys being coached and the Middlesex team doing their pre-season warm-up exercises. It is my favourite time of the year, with the smell of new-mown grass and the usual optimism in the air that this one will be the best season ever. Sadly, there is no longer that nostalgic smell of linseed oil to mingle with the other smells of spring. These days it seems that new bats don't need the stimulus of oil, once lovingly rubbed into them at the start of the season.

In January, when I was lucky enough to go to Australia to broadcast the fifth Test at Sydney, I found some interesting developments, both on television and radio. Channel 9, the television station run by the Kerry Packer Organization, puts on a fantastic technical display, with its eight cameras and numerous gimmicks. Personally, I prefer my cricket to be presented more simply, and without so much 'hard sell'. The BBC way is still, I think, the best.

For instance, Channel 9 does the unforgiveable and has a camera at each end of the pitch. This means that the viewer sees every ball bowled from behind the bowler's arm. This is not a natural way to watch cricket. At a cricket ground the spectator does not rush to the other end of the ground at the end of every over. He stays where he is and so has a varied view of the game, sometimes seeing the ball as do the wicket-keeper and batsman, and sometimes through the eyes of the bowler. Of course, for action replays *only*, it is essential to have a camera behind the bowler's arm at each end, in order to see more clearly catches at slip or behind the wicket, and balls leading to L B W decisions.

However, Channel 9 overplays its hand by showing some replays three or four times, often in slow motion. This undoubtedly increases the pressure on umpires, and I would certainly forbid any commentator to comment on an umpire's decision. So often one hears the Australian commentator say, 'Let's just have one more look at that in slow motion . . .' before saying what he thinks. Remember, the umpire has only a second or two to make up *his* mind! There is a lot of talk nowadays about electronic aids for umpires, or a third adjudicator sitting in the pavilion in front of a television monitor. I would be against this. Television only magnifies the mistakes that have always been made. What we need are better umpires and I would ideally be in favour of neutral umpires, as they have in every other international team sport. However, this is unlikely to come about because of the expense of transporting these umpires across thousands of miles from neutral countries. English umpires are the best, anyway, and umpiring in England would not at present be improved by this system! But it would at least remove some of the pressures on umpires faced with unreasonably partisan home crowds, which are undoubtedly common in some countries.

Commercial television in Australia is severely handicapped by having to leave the cricket immediately the last ball is bowled in each over, in order to show the commercial. This means the viewer gets no opinion about the over from a summarizer, and also misses the many interesting things that occur during a changeover, such as the captain changing his bowlers or readjusting the field. This fetish for putting on a commercial regardless of the state of the game came to a farcical climax in the fourth Test at Melbourne in December last year. At the end of an over on the last morning Australia, with their last pair together, needed just four runs to win. At this point, as usual, on came the commercial. What a time to leave a match! I was watching on the television in Sydney and I swore never to buy the product which was so rudely interrupting one of the most exciting moments I have ever seen in a Test Match. To make matters worse, there was – for once – a very quick changeover and in most of Australia Channel 9 returned to the cricket too late for the viewers to see that final ball bowled by Botham to Thomson, and the catch, missed by Tavaré but finally caught by Miller on the rebound. In Sydney we were luckier: we were back just in time to see the ball leaving Botham's hand. Of course, the viewers got their playbacks *ad nauseam*, but they had been robbed of seeing England's three-run victory 'live' as it happened. What an indictment of this crazy lust for money.

Channel 9 also goes over the top with its gimmicks before start of play, with Tony Greig crouching on the pitch in front of various instruments which tell him the temperature, the humidity, the amount of moisture in the pitch and something called 'players' comfort'. On the other hand, with its eight cameras, Channel 9 is able to pick up every catch, and show it again from various angles. But I sincerely hope that if the BBC should decide to copy anything of Channel 9's coverage, they will not be tempted to show that dreadful duck which appears on the screen and stalks the batsman who has made nought back to the pavilion.

As in England, both ABC and Channel 9 Television use old Test players as commentators, with the exception of ABC's Norman May. ABC *Radio* in general still sticks to the professional broadcaster as opposed to the ex-player.

As you will, I hope, have discovered from this book, there have always been and always will be changes in the pattern of cricket commentary since it first started fifty-six years ago. British television is, I think, now set in its use of the entirely serious professional approach. So far as radio is concerned, I have no doubt that we shall see some changes in *Test Match Special* over the next few years, with more ex-Test players joining the team. The professional broadcasters on radio used to have a big advantage over the ex-players. We could practise our art with the many three-day county matches which were broadcast regularly both during the week and on Saturday afternoons. Now the only cricket broadcasts on national radio – except for Test Matches –

are short, forty-second reports on *Sport on 2*, and the local radio coverage of John Player matches on Sunday is the only 'school' left. The only people, therefore, who get any real practice at commentary are members of the *Test Match Special* team during Test Matches. This makes it very difficult to find and cultivate new talent. It takes away the advantage the broadcaster used to have over the ex-Test player, who still has in his favour the deeper technical knowledge and experience of the first-class game.

So as the broadcasters in the present team of *T.M.S.* slowly disperse, their places could well be taken by ex-players. This will undoubtedly please a small minority of *T.M.S.* listeners who, on the evidence of an article and subsequent letters in one of the cricket magazines this winter, think that we are too chatty, too friendly, too schoolboyish and too prone to making bad jokes! We are accused of being too lighthearted and not taking the game seriously enough. As the oldest member of the team and the one with the longest experience, I must take the blame. But I'm afraid that I'm too old to change. Cricket is fun and if it ceased to be so, and I were not allowed to describe its many other attractions besides the skills and techniques, I would no longer be happy commentating and would retire. That time, inevitably, cannot be far off. But to the many faithful followers who are so kind to my friends the commentators and myself, may I just say that I should love to catch my captain's eye and be asked to have another over or two from the Pavilion End.

Brian Johnston
April, 1983